A GIFT OF LOVE

A GIFT OF LOVE

Marriage as a Spiritual Quest

ANN LINTHORST

PAULIST PRESS
New York/Ramsey/Toronto

Acknowledgments

The author is grateful for permission to reprint selections from the following works:

From DIALOGUES IN METAPSYCHIATRY by Thomas Hora. Copyright © 1977 by The Seabury Press, Inc. Used by permission. From CHRISTOTHERAPY by Bernard J. Tyrell. Copyright © 1975 by the author. Used by permission of The Seabury Press, Inc. From DISCOVER THE POWER WITHIN YOU by Eric Butterworth. Copyright © 1968 by the author. Used by permission of Harper and Row, Inc. From TOWARD A PSYCHOLOGY OF BEING, 2nd ed., by Abraham Maslow © 1968 by Litton Educational Publishing, Inc. Reprinted by permission of D. Van Nostrand Company. Exerpts from THE THREE PILLARS OF ZEN by Philip Kapleau. Copyright © 1965 by Philip Kapleau. To be published in a revised edition by Doubleday & Company, Inc. Used by permission. From WHOLE CHILD, WHOLE PARENT, by Polly Berrien Berends. Copyright © 1975 by the author. Used by permission of Harper & Row, Inc. From EXISTENTIAL METAPSYCHIATRY by Thomas Hora. Copyright © 1977 by The Seabury Press, Inc. Used by permission. From THE WAY OF LIFE ACCORDING TO LAO TZU, trans. by Witter Bynner. Permission granted by Harper and Row, Inc.

Bible quotations are from the Revised Standard Version or the King James Version. A complete list of the principles of metapsychiatry is contained in the book *Dialogues in Metapsychiatry* by Thomas Hora, in Chapter 47, p. 230. Also be advised that the names of individuals in the examples have been changed.

Library of Congress
Catalog Card Number: 79-53953

ISBN: 0-8091-0302-8

Published by Paulist Press
Editorial Office: 1865 Broadway, New York, N.Y. 10023
Business Office: 545 Island Road, Ramsey, N.J. 07446

Printed and bound in the
United States of America

Contents

1. Marriage as an Alternative Life Style

"The meaning and purpose of life is to come to know Reality." [1] *"And ye shall know the truth, and the truth shall make you free"* (John 8:32).

The young people in front of me were "nothing special" and that's what was so remarkable about them. They were so much like so many other couples on the brink of divorce: hurt, bitterness, anger flashing between them, mutual accusations and complaints the stuff of their communication.

The man wanted the marriage to continue, and he kept trying to wring out of his wife an agreement to "give it a try" with demands, arguments, threats, all manner of manipulations, each maneuver simply demonstrating the unwitting tyranny from which his wife sought to escape. The woman was adamant in her decision to split and to win custody of their small son. "I've already given it a try," she kept saying. By that she meant that she had been trying to get him to change ever since they married by nagging, sulking, shouting, withholding sex and threatening divorce.

---

1. Thomas Hora, *Dialogues in Metapsychiatry*, New York: Seabury Press, 1977, motto.

Well, no more, she had had it; she was leaving. And, if that happened to deprive him of living with his son, that was just too bad. It was his own fault.

Neither individual could spare a moment to listen to anything which did not confirm his or her opinions. Neither one could even consider his or her own part in the wretched drama which had engulfed their lives. And, in spite of all the pain and discord, both seemed to take the situation somehow for granted. After all, their next-door neighbor had just gone through a divorce, as had many of their friends. It was unpleasant, but it was not in any way remarkable. That, to me, is the remarkable thing about the marriage situation in our day: that so much marital misery is considered to be unremarkable.

I felt a deep surge of anger—not at the young couple, struggling and suffering before me, but at the ideas which are the real villains in the picture: the beliefs abroad in our culture—so troublesome and illness-producing—yet so taken-for-granted that the ghastly farce being enacted before my eyes passes unquestioned, considered by multitudes to be "just the way things are" these days.

People blame one another, mostly, for the problems. Or they blame marriage and seek for an alternative form of relationship. Or they blame cultural trends—the rootlessness of our society, and so forth. But none of the blaming helps very much. As a result, couples, young, middle-aged and old, continue to struggle with one another and to suffer the disruption of their marriages. And children, by the hundreds of thousands, continue to suffer the disruption of their lives.

And it does not have to be. That was the real meaning of my anger that day: the knowledge that the struggle and suffering and disruption do not have to be. They are not a consequence of uncontrollable social forces or irremedial human traits; they are the manifestation of ideas, beliefs, which can be seen and understood and changed. And so came the decision to write this book.

It is glaringly evident that marriage is in trouble, these days, in our country. But the meaning of that trouble is not so evident. It is not simply due to a lack of social, family and religious pressures to hold marriages together, though it may seem that way because without those "glues" to keep the facades of marriage stuck together, we can see more clearly what is going on. Marriage is in trouble because it is based upon beliefs about life and people and marriage which are limited and faulty. They do not adequately represent the truth of being—the way things really are. So they don't work very efficiently or harmoniously or beautifully or healthily for us. A marriage based upon faulty information about life doesn't function any better than does an airplane built on the basis of faulty information about aerodynamics. Tinkering with the airplane is of no avail unless and until the laws of aerodynamics are correctly understood. And tinkering with marriage is of no avail until the laws of life are understood.

If we know where the real trouble lies, then the crisis in marriage and family life does not have to be a bad thing. Like all crises, it is an opportunity to learn and grow, and anyone interested in learning something may profit a great deal. Indeed, the particular difficulties of marriage in our day are fraught with unusual potential for good, because of the fact that the kind of understanding which is required for the genuine healing of marriages is "existential" understanding, that is, understanding more clearly and accurately what is true about existence. That sort of understanding not only heals marriages, it is life-enhancing and health-producing on all levels of one's life experience.

And so, the concern of the book is twofold. It is, first of all, to point to and expose the pathogenic popular beliefs which wreak so much havoc in the marital situation, for, unmasked, they lose their pretense to reality; disdained, they lose their power to harm. Secondly, the concern is to share, in the context of marriage, the principles of living which offer us all the opportunity to become seekers rather than sufferers. And those appear to be our two basic options in life and in marriage: sufferers or seekers. The principles are stated in the form of principles of metapsychiatry as formulated by Dr. Thomas Hora, for that is the form which has proven to be of daily benefit in my own life.

When I first began treatment in metapsychiatry some years ago, two things happened: I got launched on the spiritual path, and I got married. The marriage represented a healing of what had been a major conflict in my life up to that point, and that healing was a consequence of my growing spiritual interest and understanding. Through the years, the remarkable practicality of the spiritual principles of metapsychiatry in nurturing both spiritual growth and marital harmony has been consistently demonstrated. My husband Jan and I have found our marriage to be a joint quest for enlightenment in which the marriage aids and abets our spiritual growth and in which the spiritual quest undergirds and strengthens and heals the marriage.

Out of this personal experience has evolved the basic thesis of this book, which is that something very peculiar has happened in our day: the path of the spiritual seeker and the path of the marital seeker converge in a way heretofore quite unknown. The marital crisis requires that we let the spiritual dimension of reality—that is to say, God—out of the religious closet. Seeing our lives in a transcendental context is no longer a matter of religious preference; it is an existential necessity.

Marriage is where the flaws in the popular world-view of our culture pinch and pain most acutely. The basic flaw, one which we shall be examining at length throughout the book, is the belief in and worship of the human ego as the ultimate reality about man. Ego-centered living works poorly in general; in marriage it becomes unendurable for many people. And so we become interested in finding life on a higher, healthier plane; we become seekers of a trans-ego, or transcendental, consciousness of reality, and thereby we join the quest of spiritual seekers through the ages.

Marriage in our day is a very good context for the spiritual quest; it is a school for enlightenment par excellence. The healing of our marriage problems requires that we become seekers of spiritual Reality.

The convergence of concern of those seeking a solution to marital difficulties and those seeking individual spiritual growth and enlightenment via various forms of prayer and meditation is not at all evident to most of the people involved in these quests. On the contrary, in some meditation circles, it is commonly said, "Meditate and separate," pointing to the frequency of marital disruption growing out of total involvement in meditation practices. It is traditional in most thinking about the spiritual quest to regard the requirements of marriage and family life as so distracting that they effectively prevent an individual's steady growth toward higher levels of consciousness.

Likewise, the thrust in much current marriage counseling and the numerous marriage-improvement workshops which abound is based upon psychological thinking, which heightens the focus on separate, individual egos trying to get along with each other. It seems to go unrecognized that this kind of thinking is in conflict with the definition of man in spiritual terms. The wholehearted embracing of psychological thinking and methods by the major religious groups of our culture reveals a failure to think through the crucial differences in the views of man underlying psychological and spiritual concerns. Psychological thinking tends to reinforce views of reality which obstruct the spiritual seeker's growth in the direction of transcending the limitations of ego-consciousness.

In metapsychiatry, however, the marriage quest and the spiritual quest become one. The spiritual seeker is brought "down to earth" and the marriage seeker taken "up to heaven" in the discovery that what will heal the marriage and bring harmony and joy to family life is also that which elevates consciousness to an awareness of divine Reality. "All problems are psychological; all solutions are spiritual."[2]

Metapsychiatry consistently views marriage in an existential framework, that is, as necessarily related to our understanding of what life is all about. We cannot know what marriage is and how it works until we know what life is and how it works. We begin with the question "What is life?" if we want to come to a valid understanding of marriage. There are many answers to that question, but for our purposes the most relevant is: Life is a school. It is not an academic school, for the purpose of cramming our heads with facts; it is an existential school, in which we learn to see, more and more clearly, Reality. "The meaning and purpose of life is to come to know Reality."

Most people are quite unaware that they do not know Reality. It is common to assume that Reality is whatever someone thinks it is and thus is an entirely individual matter. Truth is seen as "whatever is true for me," and it follows that "nobody can tell me what is true for me." We do, all, have our individual, inner dramas, based upon ideas formed from early experiences. We'll discuss these in subsequent chapters. Nonetheless, there is Reality, a Way Things Are, a Fundamental Order of Existence, and this Reality is lawful and therefore discoverable and testable by

2. *Ibid.*, p. 68.

everyone. Just as the proof that one has correctly understood the laws of aerodynamics lies in the safe, harmonious functioning of the airplane, so the proof that one has correctly understood the laws of existence lies in the safe, harmonious functioning of one's life, on all levels and in all dimensions.

When things are not going well with someone, then, it is an indication that some faulty idea needs to be corrected, or some limited view needs to be expanded so that something more can be seen about life. That is nothing to be ashamed of; it is the nature of the human condition. We do not, any of us, start out knowing Reality. Worse, we also do not start out realizing that we do not know Reality. We are all subject to both negative and positive ignorance: that is, to a lack of understanding and to misunderstanding. The latter is the most troublesome. If someone does not know how to get somewhere and knows that he/she does not know, it is not a very difficult problem. He/she can get a map or ask someone who has been there and find out. But if he/she thinks that he/she knows and is mistaken, it may take a long time, many fruitless miles, and perhaps even untoward experiences before he/she can discover, and acknowledge, his/her mistake, and be open to right directions.

And so it is with life. Sometimes it takes a lot of hard knocks before we can ask if there is something we need to learn. Some people never get to the point of asking the question at all. The really sad thing about the opening scene was not that the couple were experiencing disharmony. It was that in their eagerness to be proven "right" and to blame the other for the difficulties, neither was anywhere near the point of asking the only really fruitful question, i.e., "Is there something for me to learn in all this?" The absence of that question foretells more miles on the wrong road and hard knocks along the way.

But if we can discover that life is a school, wherein we can correct our faulty understanding and expand our awareness to see more and more of the non-tangible dimensions of Reality, we are on the right track. Then, no matter what comes along, we will be able to learn and profit from it. And our lives will get safer and more harmonious and healthier and better all around.

Now, if this is true about life, then it is true about marriage as well. If coming to know Reality is what life is all about, then marriage cannot be about something else altogether. This is one of the big problems in the current thinking about marriage. It is viewed without context, not even the context of one's whole life, let alone the context of ultimate Reality. It is seen as something separate—a relationship, a social structure, an interpersonal contract—which can be defined, analyzed, tinkered with and perhaps made to work right, no matter what the basic views and values of the partners may be.

Underlying this idea is a culture-wide tendency to think operationally and externally about life. Here the basic world-view begins to be visible. In it, human beings are all alone inside their skins, vulnerable to what happens to them from the outside and consequently preoccupied with how to make it all go right. Ours is a "how-to" society in the extreme. (We even have a noted religious leader purporting to tell us "how to be born again" as if that were something we could do.)

Marriage is viewed as something happening to us (or not happening) and there is a focus on how to make happen what we want to happen and how to prevent from happening what we don't want to happen. These ideas are clearly not working well, and we'll explore them and their unhappy fruits in detail as we go along. For now we need only see that the trouble in our marriages is a sign that there are some lessons to be learned. If life is a school, then marriage is a school. There is no way to escape unscathed from the necessity to understand Reality, just as there is no way to escape unscathed from the necessity to understand the law of gravity. We may divorce our spouses, live together without a marriage certificate, join a commune or become a loner. But the negative consequences of our faulty understanding of life will follow us wherever we are.

Consider, for example, Janet and Harvey. The kids are grown now, and Harvey wants out of the marriage. He thinks Janet is his problem. He has, over the years, cherished the idea of himself as the "strong and good" partner, taking care of his wife, who was always subject to anxiety, dissatisfaction, dependency, and emotional disturbance, and who called him "a saint." Janet, who wants Harvey to stay, thinks he is her solution, even though, over the years, she has been so preoccupied with her mental and emotional concerns that there has been little mutuality. She cannot understand "what happened" that Harvey, the "glue" of her life, now wants out. Neither individual appears to have any idea that there might be something to be learned in all this, only that the problem could be solved by getting rid of—or hanging onto—the other person. Harvey wants his "freedom" which he thinks separating from Janet will give him. Janet wants "intimacy" which she thinks staying with Harvey could give her—if only he would give it, which he won't. But, if we look at the issues from an existential point of view, what do we find?

We find that Harvey is not imprisoned by Janet but rather by his assumption that he is in the world to be the "strong and good one" (which, of course, requires someone else to be the "weak and bad" one). He sees life as basically interpersonal and consequently imprisoning. Experiencing the negative fruits of that mental setup, Harvey thinks that he can escape from them by escaping from his wife. But Harvey needs to know that freedom is an existential issue, not an interpersonal one. Janet can neither give nor take away his freedom. Freedom can only be realized in consciousness. The only genuine freedom there is is freedom from those old, false, endlessly troublesome views of life which underlie and manifest themselves in our problems. We need the freedom to see what really is and to be— and allow others to be—what we, and they, really are.

Likewise, Janet is incapable of the very intimacy she is pursuing. Her ideas about herself and life keep her so tense, anxious, depressed and compulsively seeking relief that intimacy is impossible. Moreover, her idea of intimacy is mistaken. It is not something someone else can give her. Intimacy happens when two or more human beings share, deeply, in a moment, a oneness of understanding, appreciation, joy, peace, and goodness. Thus it, too, is an existential and not an interpersonal issue. What Janet needs is to come to know Reality so that she will be capable of understanding, joy, appreciation and peace. The sharing of them with others will then take care of itself.

A marriage cannot be healthy and harmonious unless the partners are healthy and in harmony with life, and that cannot happen unless they are interested in Reality. A concern to know Reality is essential to the healthy unfoldment of our marriages.

There is necessarily a process of learning in life, or, better, a process of the expansion of consciousness. Jesus said, "Truly, truly I say to you, unless one is born anew (from above), he cannot see the kingdom of God. . . .That which is born of the flesh is flesh, and that which is born of the Spirit is spirit" (John 3:3, 6). The physical process of a tiny baby growing into an adult and the mental process of an infant mind developing into a mature intellect may be seen as paradigms of the process in consciousness which is the essence of human development: a limited awareness expanding to an enlightened consciousness, one which can "see the kingdom of God." That's what human existence if all about.

The toddler at the beach at sunset, surrounded by a vast panorama of sky and sea, cannot see it. He is totally preoccupied with the pebble, the wavelet at his feet. His eyes can see it all, but his consciousness cannot recognize beauty, grandeur, vastness, order, harmony, all the formless realities which make such a scene so breathtaking. However, he is capable of growing into an appreciation of these things; indeed, he must do so if he is to fulfill his potential. That expansion of consciousness to the realization of aesthetic and, finally, transcendental values is the essence of our human growth process.

And yet, essential though it is, the expansion of consciousness is not an unimpeded process for anyone. We all get stuck on "pebbles." The trouble is that we grow up in a mental climate which is saturated with mistaken ideas. All of us are born into, grow up and live in, a mental world which is based upon mistaken premises about Reality, premises which spring from the chronic human practice of "judging by appearances." This vast, mental mistake-reservoir is termed, in metapsychiatry, "the sea of mental garbage." The term "garbage" is useful because it prevents equivocation on the merits of mistaken premises. Even though it may take on the appearance of something desirable, pleasurable, and "good," a mistake is always a mistake and, like garbage, it is guaranteed to stink, eventually.

Human consciousness is inevitably impeded in its process of expansion by the mental "stuff" in which it develops. From our earliest years, we pick out and identify with certain particular ideas from the "sea," and those ideas then become very, very precious to us, because we believe them to be the truth about ourselves. These ideas, which make up that sense of self which we term "the ego," become the mental "pebbles" which preoccupy us and capture our attention and interest, blinding us to the "blazing sunset" of the larger Reality.

The cost of our limited seeing becomes very clear when we look at marriage. Marriage, in our culture, is a totally ego-dominated scene. All the popular components of marriage, both positive and negative—romantic love, interpersonal relationships and intimacy, pursuit of sexual gratification, feelings of frustration, limitation, burden, being trapped, etc.—all that goes into marriage in our day and culture presupposes the ultimate Reality and validity of an ego-view of human beings: "I am what I feel and think. It is my absolute right in life to 'look out for number one.' " That's what is generally believed. And in that framework of thought, marriage is for the purpose of "getting my ego-needs met." The young couple described at the beginning were both totally ruled by the pursuit of what they wanted for themselves, and that made them blind to everything, and everybody, else. And they have the support of popular belief reinforcing that pursuit . . . and that blindness.

Even so, we are finding out, also as a culture, that ego-centered living doesn't work well in marriage and family life. Now that marriages have to survive on their intrinsic merit, rather than from various social pressures, many of them don't. Life is very tough for an ego, any ego, and when two or more of them try to live together, full-time, over the long haul, there is no escape from the painful consequences of egotistical living. If we cannot settle for the suffering, we have three choices: get out, go crazy (which is another way of getting out), or learn something. So, marriage provides a superior setting for existential learning.

In metapsychiatry, marriage is defined as "a spiritual partnership; a joint participation in the good of God." The definition itself elevates consciousness far beyond the ordinary idea of marriage as two egos, and two bodies, getting together and interacting. It makes clear from the start that life is basically spiritual, and that the good of our lives, and marriages, comes from a participation in a larger good of which we are not the authors. Thus, to become interested in marriage according to that definition sets one on a path of spiritual seeking. It requires considerable growth in consciousness just to understand, let alone actualize, marriage in these terms.

In such a marriage, the partners willingly accept their life together as a fruitful learning experience. They do not marry, or stay married, because of the good feelings and ego gratification which they are getting, or hope to get, out of the relationship. They marry in order to participate with others in the process of coming to know Reality so that they may participate with others in the good of God. Such a focus makes marriage itself an "alternative life style" compared to the popular conception of marriage, a much more radical alternative than that brought about by simply changing the structure.

A clear understanding of the existential context for marriage establishes the alternate path. When everything in marriage and family life is seen within an existential context, then everything that comes up, from sex to taking out the trash, can be an exercise in coming to know Reality rather than a battleground between two egos.

The existential concern is beautifully described by Rabbi Nachmann of Bratzlav:

> As the hand held before the eye conceals the greatest mountain, so the little earthly life hides from the glance the enormous lights and mysteries of which the world is full, and he who can draw it away from before his eyes, as one draws away a hand, beholds the great shining of the inner worlds.

The goal, then, of marriage, is not a "good marriage" in conventional terms, not good communication, for the marriage to "work" or whatever, but rather it is the enhancement of the spiritual growth of the family members. The goal is the goal of life: to know Reality, to "behold the great shining of the inner worlds." Seeing marriage as a pathway to enlightenment rather than as an arena for the gratification of egos allows it to become a continuing process of mutual helpfulness and sharing, playfulness, joy, and ever-unexpected good.

If the suffering of ego-centered marriage drives us to God, surely the enjoyment of valid living in a family setting draws us to God. Marriage is a wonderful setting within which to participate in the good of God. To paraphrase an old nursery rhyme, we might say about marriage that when it is bad, it is very bad, but when it is good, it is superb. The positive fruits of this understanding of marriage will be spelled out as we investigate the principles which lead to enlightenment and bring harmony to our lives together.

SUMMARY

- Popular belief says that life is a battleground of egos struggling to get their needs met. Marriage is for the purpose of mutual ego-gratification. This view is pathogenic, breeding discord.

- The purpose of life is to come to see Reality; to grow in consciousness to an awareness of the transcendental-spiritual nature of existence.

- This growth is blocked by our attachment to our ego-views of things.

- In marriage, this ego-orientation causes great pain and trouble. Therefore, marriage provides us with the opportunity and motivation to seek beyond the ego.

• Seekers of marital harmony thus become seekers of spiritual Reality; seekers of spiritual Reality can find marriage an excellent "school for enlightenment."

• In metapsychiatry, marriage is defined as "a spiritual partnership; a joint participation in the good of God." Marriage, so defined, is itself an "alternative life style."

2. God:
The Transcendental
Context of Human Life . . .
and Marriage

"For in him we live and move and have our being" (Acts 17:28).

When we think about our lives, and our marriages, we think about them in a certain framework of ideas which forms the context of our thinking. In other words, how we think about something—the questions we ask, the answers we get, our interpretations of events—depends upon certain basic assumptions which we hold, perhaps without even being aware of them. These assumptions are very important to us because they determine what our questions and answers and experiences are going to be. We will not be able to discover anything really new, that is, anything which does not fit in with our context of thinking, unless we become aware of the context and the automatic limitations which it imposes upon us.

The context of thought in our culture at this time is

pre-eminently that of the autonomous ego. Heightened enormously by the development of both technological and psychological thinking, the idea that human beings are separate, autonomous, skin-encapsulated egos reigns supreme. Whenever we think about ourselves or our affairs, it is in the context of this belief about the nature of human life. And, since we experience what we believe, everything seems to confirm to us that this is the way things really are. We are all alone, wrapped up inside our skins, having to live out of the resources contained inside the wrapper and vulnerable to all that goes on outside of the wrapper. In the image of a Zen koan, or riddle, a human being is a "goose in a bottle."

That is clearly a difficult situation in which to be. The consequences of that idea are not hard to trace. Being a "goose in a bottle" means that we are limited to a given amount of personal resources: intellectual, physical and emotional, which seem to be distributed unevenly and quite arbitrarily. Moreover, our initial environments appear to be distributed in the same manner. Since we are vulnerable to that which happens outside of us, the environmental distributions seem to be as basically incomprehensible, if not unjust, as our congenital differences.

We believe that the thoughts and feelings "inside our skins" constitute our true being, so we are driven to defend those thoughts and feelings as if our lives depended upon them. We are equally driven to try to manage other people and external circumstances so that they do not "damage" us in any way and, hopefully, so that they may even provide us with what we think we need, i.e., whatever makes us feel good, safe, O.K. A skin-encapsulated ego is necessarily limited, burdened, anxious and resentful.

Naturally, we develop ways, both individually and culturally, of trying to make ourselves as comfortable as possible within our troublesome context. The popular ideas show up in the form of popular songs, and songs that extol the importance of "being me" and doing things "my way" reveal that one popular way to try to get as comfortable as a goose in a bottle is to glorify the sense of separateness and distinctness. The other currently popular form is reflected in a song which declares that we are very "lucky" if we "need" other people. We can also glorify the idea of inter-personal dependency in an attempt to ease our sense of isolation. But the fact remains that a goose in a bottle is always isolated, limited and longing to be free.

It is very helpful to know that this idea about the nature of things is only an idea and not the unchangeable structure of Reality. It is also very helpful to know that our basic feelings of isolation, limitation and imprisonment are a consequence of this mistaken idea, unwittingly picked up from the mental climate (the sea of mental garbage) in which we live, and are not the consequence of our spouse's behavior, our own personalities, having children, or any of the other common targets of blame.

It is very popular these days for both husbands and wives to "drop out" of their marriages as a consequence of the belief that the marriage is robbing them of their personal fulfillment. Feelings of frustration, lack, resentment at the demands of family life, etc., are attributed to the marriage itself and its details. Several years ago, I read in the alumni notes of my college something like this:

> I left my husband, four children, two dogs, two cars, a job as an executive secretary and a big home in the suburbs to come and live with my lover under an apricot tree in a tiny trailer. I did it for the same reason I originally went to college: in order to find freedom, identity, self-actualization.

Would that she could leave her ego behind in the suburbs with the family. Then dropping out would be a real solution. But it just doesn't happen that way. We take our ego-consciousness with us wherever we go, and it causes trouble wherever we are, whether we live in a trailer or a mansion.

The basic problem is believing that one is an ego. When we try to live life in a context bounded by the contours of our skins and going no higher than the tips of other people's heads, there are a number of negative side-effects which cannot be eliminated by any of our management techniques, frantically-pursued distractions or psychological sophistication.

Indeed, psychology has greatly increased the difficulty of living with this view of Reality. It is psychology which has indentified—and deified—the ego, leading us to believe that our true selves are to be found in that welter of distorted ideas, false concerns and deceptive emotions which "lie within." It's bad enough to have to manage the entire universe, outside of one's skin, without having also to manage a complex inner world peopled by such figures as "the id," "the inner child," and "the internal saboteur." It has been said that one is, psychologically, a group rather than an individual. Talking about ideas as if they were people does no service to anyone, and the ego consists of ideas, nothing more. Seeing oneself as a goose in a bottle is problematic; seeing oneself as several geese in a bottle is worse.

Predictably, a great deal of marriage and family counseling participates in the problem rather than solving it, by continuing to assume the ego-context for family life. Conventional marriage counseling is rife with such phrases as "getting in touch with your feelings," "learning to fight fair," "negotiating problem issues," "making contracts," and many others which reveal clearly the idea that a family is made up of individual egos struggling with themselves and each other for survival and comfort.

For example, Mary and John had had some months of marriage counseling. Although they were both very bright, ambitious and creative people with "everything going" for them and their two young children, they feared that they were on the brink of divorce. Incessant bickering, culminating in lengthy, bitter verbal battles, seemed to indicate to them that they just couldn't make it together. In marriage counseling, they had learned to limit their fights to one-half hour and to negotiate on the problem issues; he agreed to be with the family one night a week and weekends if she would stop nagging. But when John was home, he seemed withdrawn and preoccupied, and that frustrated Mary almost more than his absence. She had learned to be in touch with her feelings and was furious because he didn't seem to be. He was intellectual and logical in his approach to things and resentful because she was unable to be. Although their fights stayed within the prescribed limits, Mary despaired. She said, "I just couldn't see that anything basic had changed." She was, of course, absolutely right.

Thinking in an ego context, Mary saw her problem as being John's apparent disinterest in the home, that is, in her and the kids. Taking his behavior personally, she felt put down by his preoccupation with his work and activities. Her mind was filled with what he should do and should not do in order to reassure her, make her feel good about herself, etc. His consistent violation of her "shoulds" made her frantic and led her to all sorts of extremes to try to make him conform. John, whose entire sense of competence was invested in his reasoning capacities, which were paying off substantially in the growth of his business but which were seemingly useless and unappreciated at home, saw Mary as emotional, irrational and harassing. No matter what her ploy—tears, rage, demands that they "talk about" their problems—he felt attacked and retreated into the invincible armor of his intellectual reasoning. They were two "gooses in bottles" whose ways of trying to manage their own ego-discomforts provoked greater discomforts in one another and led them to believe that the only solution was to separate. Their pain and their attempts to relieve it are commonplace in our culture, endemic to our world-view.

So what's an ego to do? That's always the question: what to do. How can we possibly know what to do until we understand what the real problem is? The problem, in this case, was the ego context of their thinking. In other words, the problem was their unknowing commitment to certain mistaken ideas. The solution, then, lies in knowing something. We all need to know that human beings are not isolated egos, struggling with internal and external management problems. A human being is, rather, "an 'image and likeness of God,' or, preferably, a manifestation of cosmic Love-Intelligence . . . capable of attaining higher levels of consciousness and of beholding Reality in its spiritual dimension."[1]

Knowing that gives us a new context for our thinking. God is, in reality, the context of our lives, our being. That's what the term "God" means. It means that we live in a context larger than that of ego-consciousness. The old argument over the existence of God is based upon a rather primitive view of God as a sort of Super Somebody Somewhere. Only if we understand God in limited, personal terms can we possibly argue about whether or not he exists. The real, existential question underlying that false argument is one everybody asks in some way: "What is the nature of life?" We don't argue about whether or not existence exists or being bes. We exist. We be. What we want to know is: What is it all about?

1. Thomas Hora, *Dialogues in Metapsychiatry, op. cit.,* p. 1

Actually, the term "God" is a statement about the nature of reality. It says that we live in a transcendental, spiritual context and derive our being, identity, life and resources from that larger context. It says that we are participants in a Reality which transcends us all and sets the terms—existential laws—which govern our lives. And because Reality is lawful it is testable, provable. One need not argue at all. Anyone interested may demonstrate in his own life-experience the reality of the transcendental context and the spiritual laws which govern it. The proof lies in the life-enhancing and health-producing effects of living and thinking in a God-context rather than an ego-context. We'll try it out, as we go along, in connection with marriage.

The place to begin is with the affirmation that God is the context for our lives and consequently for our marriages. Affirming that, we can see that there is a need to refer, constantly, to that context in our thinking about whatever comes up in marriage. No matter how fervent our belief in God and how dedicated our participation in religious structures, if our views about life and ourselves and our marriages are not being transformed by a continual process of referring to—seeing the situation in—the context of transcendental Reality, then we stand up being "closet atheists." Secretly, we live without reference to God, in an ego context, and our belief in God will not save us from the consequences of that false context.

What does it mean to refer to God in all matters of our lives? It does not mean just saying some words directed to that Super Somebody Somewhere and then going on about things the same old way. It means being concerned to understand what is going on in the light of our being— actually, manifestations of cosmic Love-Intelligence. Our situation is not at all what it appears to be. The ego defines our selves and our situations on the basis of limited and erroneous information, and we need to stop listening to and believing those "voices" (thoughts) which pour from it incessantly, keeping us involved in the "sea of mental garbage." Jesus advised, "Do not judge by appearances, but judge with right judgment" (John 7:24). Thinking in the context of God enables us to rightly judge—see—the actuality of our situation.

Human beings are actually individual manifestations of those qualities which make up perfect Life. There are not two kinds of Life: God's perfect, spiritual Life and then the life of individuals, material, limited, lacking, crippled, distorted, ugly, evil or otherwise flawed. "God don't make no trash." There is only Life; it is essentially non-corporeal, though it manifests itself in an infinite variety of forms, and it always consists of the same "stuff": love, intelligence, beauty, harmony, goodness. Life is God and always includes all the qualities of divine Reality. The life of human beings, seen as "images and likenesses" of God, is that same Life, made up of that same "stuff." So, a human being is made up of spiritual qualities. And secretly, somehow, we know that. We know that life is only valuable, i.e., real life, to the degree that it partakes of those qualities.

Yet very often we do not realize the truth of our lives because of our ego-context thinking. To the ego, life is experiences, and the more untoward the better. The ego is driven continually to confirm itself: "I am, and I am of Ultimate Importance." Every ego wants to be center stage, spotlight, and there's no better role for that purpose than that of tragic hero or tragic heroine. Just watch your ego and you'll notice this. If your spouse makes what you consider to be an unkind remark, just watch your ego blow it up. Why be just slightly abused when you can savor the idea of being the most abused husband or wife in the world? Notice how the ego can't resist going over and over a supposed slight or other minor disharmony. Think of the vast popularity of stories about people dying of terminal diseases. A loving father once told me, in great distress and embarrassment, of his repeated fantasies that his little girl died and he was the object of the enormous sympathy of many people. Ego life is a series of experiences in which one's self is in the spotlight. It's easy to see why we don't ordinarily realize the goodness, beauty and harmony of our true being and life.

Nonetheless, the Life that we live—or, perhaps we should say, that lives us—is spiritual and whole. We are in this world to bloom, to make manifest the qualities of that Life fully, in the particular, unique form which constitutes each one's individuality. The image is somewhat limited, but it may be helpful to think of a stained-glass window which, without light, is dark and colorless, but which, as a transparency to the light, comes into fullest, most beautiful expression. Life cannot bloom apart from the qualities or values which are its basic nature. And this means that your life cannot unfold in a fruitful and happy and healthy way apart from the love and intelligence, reverence, joy, harmony, goodness, beauty, gratitude and other values which are the actual "stuff" of real life.

What does this have to do with marriage? Well, marriages bloom the same way individuals do. Yet because the cultural picture of marriage is so totally ego-oriented, we are fooled into trying to make things go right in a way which actually blocks the flow of the good we are seeking. In trying to get what we think we need for ourselves, we very often live in unintelligent, unloving, irreverent, dishonest ways, disregarding harmony and order, ignoring beauty and goodness . . . and then we wonder why things don't go right for us.

Mary and John, each concentrating on trying to get "what I want" and "what makes me feel good," were, unknowingly, behaving in very unloving, unintelligent, self-defeating ways. When it was suggested to them that, instead of thinking in terms of how they feel, what they want, or who is right (and who is wrong), they each consider the question "What is the loving and intelligent response to this situation?" Mary was amazed. She caught on right away and found that it made things so simple and easy to resolve. John had a bit more difficulty at first because it was so important to him to "be right," and he asked, "But whose idea of what is loving and intelligent do we go by?" That question was very helpful because it revealed the importance of the transcendental context in our thinking.

Love and intelligence and goodness and beauty and honesty are not personal attributes or personal possessions, but universal realities which "belong only to God" and in which we may participate as channels. We do not originate these values and cannot take personal credit for them. But we may cherish them and choose to identify with and express them. Most importantly, we can reverence the transcendental Source of these life-enhancing and health-producing qualities. We can love God, which is done by beholding and being grateful for all good. When this is the state of our consciousness, then we receive, through inspiration, wisdom: loving and intelligent ideas which resolve things without ego-conflict. It is always God's idea of what is loving and intelligent that supplies our needs.

When John got over a desire to think up and take credit for ideas about what is loving and intelligent and became willing to let Love-Intelligence manifest itself in his thinking and living, it made a big difference. The unsolvable became solvable; there was greater harmony and much less rage and frustration. Seeking solutions from a Source beyond the self (outside the bottle) already tends to dissolve the sense of being "at loggerheads" which is so unyielding in a self versus self approach. For John and Mary, the sharp sense of being unable to live together faded and was replaced by a sense of confidence in their ability to live and work together constructively.

Formal prayer and meditation practices are obviously ways of making one's consciousness available to the inspired wisdom or creative intelligence which harmonizes and unfolds our lives. We will discuss in detail in later chapters some forms and practices of prayer and meditation in the family setting. It is important for spiritual seekers to realize, however, that the effect of these times apart will be greatly minimized if they spend all the rest of the day thinking and acting within an ego-context.

The continual attempt to refer to an existential context in one's daily affairs is itself a very potent form of meditation. God is not in any way abstract or irrelevant to our daily concerns. On the contrary, God is relevant to the nitty-grittiest of issues, such as taking out the trash. It seems as if taking out the trash, as a marital issue, is almost a national institution. When we married, my husband, who is Dutch, was given a package of trash bags by his friends, who advised him, "You'd better learn right now that in America husbands have to take out the trash." It is simply amazing to hear couples talk about their inability to resolve the issue of taking out the trash.

The scene usually goes as follows. The wife thinks it is the husband's job, and the husband has agreed to do it. Yet, week after week, he does not get it done when she thinks he should, and she begins to nag. He resists the nagging by putting it off even longer, she begins to get upset, there is a fight, and eventually he takes it out in a rage, she takes it out in a rage, or they both, in a rage, let it sit. The anger and resentment carry over to the next day or two, poisoning the atmosphere in the home. And some couples go through this every week.

She says, "It's his fault. He agreed to do it but then he doesn't do it unless I nag him until he can't stand it. I don't like the nagging any more than he does, but he doesn't give me any choice." He says, "It's her fault. Every week, the minute I get home from work on the night before the trash truck comes, she starts in on me. I'm tired when I get home. I like to have a little breathing space, a little appreciation for the fact that I've worked hard all day. I'm just not going to jump at her command to take out the trash. I'll do it when I'm ready."

Two things are striking in this picture of the problem. One is that, of course, each individual is seeing the issue in an ego-context: "What I think, what I want." The other is that the issue of the trash is completely lost in the swamp of personal and interpersonal concerns. Not only is God absent from the picture, but even the trash is absent from the picture. And that follows. When ego is in the foreground, it always obscures the real issues. When Love-Intelligence is in the foreground, it always clarifies and illuminates the real issues.

What, then, is the real issue? It is two-dimensional. The simple issue is the trash. Trash needs to be taken out or it becomes a nuisance and, eventually, a hazard to all those living in the home. One takes out the trash because the trash needs to be taken out. There is a Zen story about a student who came before the Master, seeking enlightenment, and presumably expecting pearls of wisdom about the secret of life to fall from the Master's lips. The Master simply asked the student "Did you eat breakfast this morning?" and the student replied "Yes." "Then," said the Master, "go and wash your rice bowl." And, reportedly, the student became enlightened.

Learning to respond, moment by moment, to the simple needs of home life—to wash the dishes because they need to be washed, take out the trash because it needs to be taken out, and so forth—is a sign of considerable spiritual maturity as well as a great enhancement to family life. The ego always wants to tack on its own false issues. When it is allowed to do so, then these simple tasks get weighted down with calculative thinking and emotional reactions and become very difficult and complex. To keep the simple issue simple is a practice in ego-transcendence well worth the effort.

There is also an existential issue and need: the need of the individuals involved to be channels for those qualities which, alone, will cause their lives to bloom. *Who* takes out the trash is of no consequence, existentially, though it is the big issue in ego terms. That the trash gets taken out is the simple, material need; that love and intelligence and respect and harmony get expressed is the existential need.

So, the wife needs to ask herself what the real issue is, and she needs to be responsive to that issue on both levels—no matter what her husband is doing or saying. Likewise, the husband needs to respond to the real issues and needs, no matter what his wife is saying or doing. (Using the other person's ignorance as an excuse for indulging in your own makes no more sense than stepping out a tenth-story window just because someone else is too ignorant to take the elevator.) It is not really difficult to respond to the real issues when we know that we are the ones who will suffer from letting ourselves get hooked by ego-concerns. To gain an ego "victory" at the cost of filling our homes with disharmony, friction, rage, frustration and resentment, when we can easily meet a simple need and at the same time invite harmony, love and intelligence into the family atmosphere, just doesn't make sense.

Mental garbage is far more hazardous than physical garbage, yet in numerous ways we consistently open the doors of our mental homes and invite the garbage man to dump his full load into our living rooms. The way we get the mental trash removed and keep our mental homes fresh and fragrant and lovely is by seeing every situation in the context of God. It is a matter of keeping in mind, in all the issues which come up, that the self, with its feelings, makes problems, but only God can solve problems. As we have noted, "All problems are psychological and all solutions are spiritual."

It is an interesting and fruitful exercise for family members, including school-age children, to make an inventory of the values which are cherished, to a greater or lesser degree, in the home. A sample inventory is provided. It is important that it be an inventory of spiritual values and not a critique of negatives. Although it is popular in some circles for couples to tell each other what "bugs" them the most about the other, this kind of practice is necessarily ego-oriented and therefore not constructive. We need to see the good, in ourselves and others and life, more and more and more. The good is always ego-transcending. We may recognize which values we need to be more mindful of, but we never take it upon ourselves to tell others what we think they need to learn.

"Home" is much more a mental climate than a physical structure. When we know that God is the context of our marriages, then our homes can be filled with those spiritual values which nurture our lives together.

SUMMARY

• The ordinary context of our lives and thinking is a belief in man as an autonomous ego: "a goose in a bottle." That is really a terrible position in which to be, and that belief, therefore, leads to feelings of isolation, anxiety, limitation, frustration, and resentment.

• The real context of life is God. The term "God" does not refer to a Giant Ego somewhere but defines the nature of Reality—*our* Reality. To talk about God is to say that things are not the way they seem to be from an ego point of view.

• There is only one kind of Life: spiritual and perfect. Man is a manifestation of that Life in individual form. If we are not to be "closet atheists," we need to constantly see ourselves and our marriages in the context of God—Reality—instead of ego.

• Seeing God as the context for our marriages means being concerned, in all matters, with the expressing of spiritual values.

FAMILY VALUES INVENTORY

Below is a list of qualities, or values. Please check those which you think are present in your family life—that is, consistently expressed by one or more family members.

Love	Appreciation	Thoughtfulness
Intelligence	Graciousness	Forthrightness
Respect	Joy	Harmony
Reverence	Peace	Beauty
Understanding	Honesty	Generosity

Now check those you would like to see *more* consistently expressed in your family life.

Love	Appreciation	Thoughtfulness
Intelligence	Graciousness	Forthrightness
Respect	Joy	Harmony
Reverence	Peace	Beauty
Understanding	Honesty	Generosity

Now check those which you think you, especially, express consistently in your family life.

Love	Appreciation	Thoughtfulness
Intelligence	Graciousness	Forthrightness
Respect	Joy	Harmony
Reverence	Peace	Beauty
Understanding	Honesty	Generosity

Now check those you would like to express more consistently in your family life.

Love	Appreciation	Thoughtfulness
Appreciation	Graciousness	Forthrightness
Respect	Joy	Harmony
Reverence	Peace	Beauty
Understanding	Honesty	Generosity

3. Marital Movies or the Only-Good Good?

"Thou shalt have no other interests before the good of God, which is spiritual" (Principle 1 of Metapsychiatry).

Principle 1 of Metapsychiatry is a paraphrasing of the first commandment: "Thou shalt have no other gods before me." What is the value of a paraphrase? In this case, it clarifies the issues, so that the relevance of the commandment to our contemporary thinking and concerns can be seen.

The principle points up two basic issues: interest and the nature of the good. Since marriage is here defined as a joint participation in the good of God, it is important that we understand clearly what that good is, and what it means to be interested in it.

The most obvious thing we can say about the good is that it is not bad. Obvious as this may seem, it is a very illuminating idea when taken seriously as a guide for thinking and living. To be interested in the good means just exactly that, and it therefore means not being interested in the bad. It is good to be interested in the good, suggests the first principle, because the good is where God is. Being interested in goodness and being interested in God go together. Jesus said, "If you, then, who are evil, know how to give good gifts to your children, how much more will your Father who is in heaven give good things to those who ask him" (Matthew 7:11). God gives good to those who ask for it, that is, who are interested in it.

The first principle offers us a guide, a standard for seeing clearly whether our thinking is on the beam or off it, and the first checkpoint is simply this: Are my thinking and experience full of goodness or badness? That simple test can help us wake up to our great need for mental house-cleaning. Many people who consider their lives to be "good" in the sense of being "normal" or "ordinary" are actually living in the existential equivalent of a sewer: their minds and experience are full of physical problems, emotional upsets, interpersonal frictions, personal lack and stress and negative mental musings. That's supposed to be real life. But it isn't, and it isn't good. The bad is bad, and the good is good, and the good is where God is. And so it is suggested that we become interested, first of all, in goodness rather than badness.

Secondly, the principle defines the good specifically as "the good of God," and here it contrasts, not with the clearly bad, but with what we shall call "the ego-good," the things which an individual's ego tells him are good. The good is that which God defines as the good, and it has clear characteristics which make it possible for us to distinguish it from what the ego defines to us as good. It is, the principle says, "spiritual." Again, taking the obvious first, "spiritual" means not material, without form. That does not mean anti-form, it just means without it. The term "spiritual" is a much-maligned concept in popular usage. For many people that word has a slightly unpleasant aroma, suggesting church and "shoulds" and trying to pretend you are not interested in material things that you really are interested in. A woman divorced from a minister and living with another man fairly bristled at the word: "For twenty years I tried to be spiritual about my lousy sex life. Finally I've got a good sex life, and I'm not interested in being spiritual about it." For her, spiritual was clearly not good.

But that is a misunderstanding of what spiritual means. The term refers to all the intangible dimensions and values of life which, far from robbing life of its robustness, in fact are the very stuff of life. Vitality, health, intelligence, harmony, joy, love, beauty, kindness, generosity, respect, reverence, peace, etc.—this is the good of God. What would life be without these things? Spiritual values are the essence of Life. They have no form of their own, yet without them the forms of material existence are lifeless and worthless. Sex without love or beauty or joy or kindness? Money without generosity, intelligence, or peace? A marriage without harmony, love, respect, or joy? Existence without spiritual values is a miserable thing, indeed. Cherishing spiritual values has nothing to do with being religious or goody-goody. Spiritual values are the quality of life.

The good of God, because it is "of God" and "spiritual," has two characteristics which contrast markedly with ego-good. It is unqualifiedly good, that is, always-good and only-good, without any negative side effects. And it is universally good: good for all individuals and available to all individuals, not just a few. It unifies people, families, neighbors, friends, co-workers, etc., rather than dividing them. Moreover, because it is without form, it is not dependent upon any particular form; forms may come and go, but the good of God is constant and unprecarious.

In marriage, the good of God provides a foundation which is a bedrock of stability. There is no better motive for marriage than a shared desire to discover together the good of God and establish a home life which manifests and participates in this spiritual quality of living. Partners who marry on such a basis, or discover such a mutual concern at some point, also find that their individual quest for the good of God is potentiated by the shared concern.

This potentiation process is one of the great joys of marriage when it is good-oriented. Each partner is particularly strong in realizing certain qualities and less aware of others. This can be very enriching for both partners. Over the years I have delighted in learning from my husband, among other things, generosity. His continual, varied expressions of it have opened my eyes to it and enabled me to realize it to a degree. And I have also delighted in seeing him discover certain other qualities and grow in them. When the quality of life is the focus of interest in a marriage, then differences tend to enrich and bring out the best in both partners; they are complementary, like a key and a lock. But a consistent interest in spiritual qualities is not the ordinary focus of interest in human affairs.

What are human beings ordinarily interested in? Elementary, my dear Watson! Themselves! The self is always most interested in itself, and this is true even when it is concerned to be unselfish. Consider the telling comment of a man who said, "I'm sick and tired of being unselfish because I'm not getting anything out of it."

There is no point in condemning oneself for being selfish. It is more helpful to understand the nature of the self, because only understanding can yield genuine selflessness, and that's what is needed. Metapsychiatry awakens us to the real "devil" in our lives: the inherent tendency of the self to confirm itself, to say, "I am and my reality is." This tendency, as it shows up in one's thought-patterns, is termed "self-confirmatory thinking" and it is easily observable by anyone who is interested in observing it. Self-confirmatory thinking refers to the incessant desire of the ego to establish its position as the center of the universe and to have confirmed as true its particular conclusions about Reality.

Human beings all make the mistake of identifying themselves as egos—separate, self-determined and self-governed lives. Consequently, until they awaken to their true identities as individual manifestations of the One Life, they are subject to a compulsive mental process of "looking out for number one." The ego feels a need to say "I am" all the time, and *what* "I am" is not important as long as it emphasizes that "I am." "I am sick . . . abused . . . poor . . . inferior, etc." are quite as effective for the purposes of self-confirmation as "I am beautiful . . . wealthy . . . famous . . . desired." The ego has no built-in standard of good; anything is good to the ego which says "I am."

The basic ego-good, then, is self-confirmation. How does self-confirmatory thinking show up in marriage? It shows up in the belief and expectation that our spouses will govern their lives in a way which will please us. Egos do not like not to be confirmed. We are uncomfortable around people who disagree with us. Marriage in our culture is based upon "love" which is really the experience of feeling super-confirmed by somebody else, and married people therefore take it for granted that they can expect their spouses to continue to confirm them, make them feel good and comfortable, throughout their marriage. Every married individual knows from experience how hard it is to let one's husband or wife behave in ways which go against one's own way of thinking and behaving. Whenever one partner fails to confirm the other's expectations or wishes in some way, there is friction, and in the long haul of marriage the friction can occur over the pettiest of issues.

Clara describes an example from her marriage:

I was reading the Bible, waiting for my husband to come in and meditate with me. He came in, but for some reason he picked up his guitar and began to play, even though he knew that I was waiting to meditate. I slammed shut the Bible and banged it down on the table. He slammed down the guitar and stamped out of the room. We still aren't speaking to each other. I can actually see that it wasn't such a terrible thing for him to play a few notes on the guitar, yet I feel that I could never, never admit that to him.

In a marriage which is governed by self-confirmatory definitions of "the good," life together becomes a series of "marital movies," interpersonal dramas, written, produced, directed by and starring the two egos of the marriage partners. The term "movies" is used to point to the essentially fictitious quality of these dramas because ego is itself a fiction, a false belief in a separate, material personhood, which deceives us into turning our lives over to the "sea of mental garbage." There is no ego, really. The "you" that you think you are does not exist. It is simply an accumulated residue of past beliefs/experiences. Man is not a self but an image and likeness of God.

When we think *we* are running our lives, it is actually old and faulty beliefs which are doing so, and then our daily experience tends to be a replay, over and over, of those same old thoughts. Just as a movie is actually completed, determined, all "on film" even as it begins to run, so our experience is already determined before it happens, as long as our thinking is governed by a belief in ego.

The marital movie described by Clara features twin inner monologues which go something like this: "He/she shouldn't have done what he/she did. It made me mad. I have a right to be mad because I was badly treated, and I'm going to stay mad until he/she says or does what I want him/her to. I'm not going to give in first because it was his/her fault." These are the thoughts underlying Clara's feeling that she could "never, never admit to" her husband that it was no big deal. To the ego, it is good if it is a big deal. And so the sulking goes on.

It is clear, in this marital movie, that both individuals, for all their Bible-reading and meditating, are more interested in self-confirmatory thinking than they are in the quality of life they are sharing. Now, if you spoke with either individual alone and asked "But aren't you interested in harmony and joy and peace?" each would of course reply "Yes," but each would also add, "But I can't do it alone. Why should I be the one to do it all? He/she has to give something, too!" So what can we observe? That, although there is a professed interest in harmony, each individual remains *more* interested in the ego-good—the drama, the bad feelings, having the spouse come across with the desired behavior—than in the good of God.

Here we can see the significance of the principle: "Thou shalt have no other interests *before* the good of God." If we are not *more* interested in the good of God than we are in anything else, then we are not interested enough for it to become actualized in our lives. Jesus' observation that "you cannot serve two masters" is usually taken as an injunction: you should not do it. But, in fact, he was pointing out that it is impossible to do it. It doesn't work. What we are most interested in governs our life-experience, like it or not.

Acknowledging our true interests is often very hard for us. We are afraid that they represent our true selves, and we therefore don't want to realize the grubbiness of our concerns. On the surface, it would seem unlikely that people would be interested in suffering. Yet when the nature of self-confirmatory thinking is understood, it becomes clear that if material lack, physical illness, interpersonal disharmony, etc., are aspects of individuals' basic assumptions about themselves and life, those individuals will unwittingly cling to their sufferings. They are *interested* in their sufferings, you see, and it is impossible to lose that which one is interested in.

Interest may take any of three forms. Cherishing, hating and fearing are all forms of interest. Whatever is cherished, hated or feared is believed in, is considered to be very important, and becomes the focus of mental preoccupation. Whatever an individual is mentally preoccupied with tends to come into his experience. This is what accounts for the patterns of experiences which are observable in everyone's life. Thus, recognizing that one is interested in something is not the same thing as saying that one likes it. A woman who is consistently beaten up by her husband doesn't like it. She hates it and fears it. But she thereby remains interested in it. And, of course, such gross physical abuse is extremely self-confirmatory. These factors account for the well-documented fact that such women find it extremely difficult to get free from such marriages and tend, if they do become free, either to find another man who will repeat the pattern or even to remarry the same abusive husband. The longer one has starred in one's particular home movie, and the more dramatic the part, the more difficult it is to turn off the projector and come out into the clear sunshine of Reality.

There is only one way out of the movie theater, and that way is God. God is Reality, and our life-experience will therefore be real only to the degree that it is God-centered. Being God-centered means continually subjecting what the ego tells us is good to the light of spiritual good and being willing to relinquish the ego-good if it proves to be invalid. "If your right eye causes you to sin, pluck it out and throw it away . . . and if your right hand causes you to sin, cut it off and throw it away" counseled Jesus (Matthew 5:29-30). No matter how dear and cherished the false belief or concern, it is not really good unless it manifests spiritual good, and painful though it may seem to give it up, it is not nearly so painful as the consequences of clinging to it.

How does one go about changing one's interest, from self-confirmation to the good of God? It is clearly not possible simply to say, "There, now, I won't be interested in myself. I'll be interested in God." It is significant that the fad, popular in some religious circles recently, of wearing a button saying "Me third," which was supposed to involve putting God first and others second, still focuses the attention on the "me." Equally fruitless is the temptation to clobber oneself mentally over the issue: "There I go again. Won't I ever learn? What a selfish person I am, what a spiritual failure, etc." A look at the "I's" in those sentences reveals how self-confirmatory it is to run oneself down.

We cannot make our interests change, but we can allow them to do so. It is something like developing an appetite for a new food. Suppose you want to learn to like vegetables, because you know that it would profit you, physically, in several ways if you ate more of them. Your attention would begin to focus on vegetables. You would probably notice the varieties of vegetables and ways of preparing them in a way you never had before. You would try out various ones, making a point of giving yourself the opportunity to develop a taste for them. Gradually, your taste for the old diet would drop away, replaced by your increasing appreciation for the new.

We need, first of all, to realize that the chronic patterns of self-confirmatory thinking, and the old ego-judgments about what is "good," are not working well for us and are, in fact, at the heart of our miserable marital movies. If we can observe ego-thinking and its consequences for us, we will be motivated to develop an appetite for something new, for spiritual nourishment rather than ego-nourishment. One of the primary concerns of this book, in spelling out, again and again, how the ego belief operates in our thinking, is to unmask the "devil" so that it is clearly discernible as the devil. Then we become free to find healthier interests. When we realize the price we pay for letting ego dictate what is "good," we become increasingly interested in a gooder-good.

The terrible suffering consequent upon a commitment to ego-goods in marriage became clear to me one Sunday when I received a phone call from a young woman—we'll call her Helen—who was in treatment with a psychologist. Here is the story she recounted:

> I'm terribly afraid, because my husband Jerry left the house with a gun in his hand. When I went into the bedroom, I found this note. It says, "I had just begun to believe that things could go right for me" (he just started a new job which he really likes) "but now everything has gone wrong. If my own wife won't talk to me, what can I expect from anyone else? Take care of the baby. I love you both." I'm afraid he's going to kill himself.
>
> It all started last night when we had a discussion about trust, and Jerry said some things that I didn't like. This morning, when we got up, I just didn't feel like talking to him—I just didn't like him right then. So I wouldn't say anything to him, and he got mad. He kept trying to get me to talk to him, but I didn't feel like it, so I just didn't say anything. He kept at me, so finally I told him, "I don't like you right now and I don't feel like talking to you." That hurt his feelings, I guess. Maybe I shouldn't have said it, but that's what I felt. Finally, he said he was going out. He wanted me to ask him to stay. But right then I didn't want him around, so I couldn't say what he wanted to hear. So he went into the bedroom and when he came out, he had the gun, and he left. And then I found the note. What shall I do?

What a Sunday morning for a young couple with a baby! What a marital movie! Fortunately I heard later that Jerry was back home and "everything was all right," but it won't stay all right unless at least one of them has learned something from the episode. These two young people nearly precipitated a dreadful tragedy because of their blind commitment to what the ego told them was "good." Helen didn't feel like talking to her husband. What were her feelings based on? On her husband's failure, the evening before, to give her what she wanted verbally: "He said some things I didn't like." Jerry was frantic, driven to nearly self-destructive extremes by ... what? By Helen's obstinacy? No, by his own refusal to let go of his demand that she give him what he wanted: talk to him, reassure him, make him feel good about himself.

The theme song of the ego in marriage was voiced in a popular song of years past: "Gimme, gimme, gimme, gimme what I cry for ... you know you made me love you." It sounds very romantic in song, but that "gimme" hurts us plenty.

Psychology would have us believe that we are egos who feed off one another, that we cannot live without interpersonal confirmation, and that, consequently, "gimme" is a valid and necessary demand. I have heard people being counseled to "learn to ask for what you want." But if we refuse to let the experts bamboozle us and we simply observe what a "gimme" orientation does to our marriages, we will find ourselves in search of a better way.

The truth is that we do not need what we want, necessarily, though we may sometimes want what we need. "I want" is the devil speaking, the voice of self-confirmatory concern. And no matter how charmingly or convincingly they present themselves, devils are no good.[1] Every ego-good has a bad side to it. Getting what we want can be the worst thing to ever happen to us.

What we need is the good of God. It alone is wholly

1. See the chapter entitled "Devils Are No Good, You Know That, Don't You?" in *The Empty Mirror* by Janwillem van de Wetering (Boston: Houghton Mifflin Co., 1975).

good, it alone blesses and unifies all concerned, and it alone satisfies not only the specific needs of the moment, on whatever levels they may arise, but in addition satisfies our existential need to know that we are whole and life is good. But just how do we relate this spiritual good to the specific issues of the moment? Like Clara and her husband, most people would undoubtedly say that they are indeed interested in harmony and joy and peace, but that they just don't find much of those things around in their marriages.

Well, the first principle gives us a clue as to why spiritual good may seem to be lacking—"no other interests before. . . ." We live what we love best of all, what comes first in our thoughts, what we are most attached to mentally. If we want good things, good experiences, good relationships in our lives, then we must love spiritual good more than anything else in the world. And if we do that, then our thoughts will be full of goodness the majority of the time. Instead of "looking out for number one" in our thoughts all the time, we will be "looking out for loveliness": seeking to see everywhere the good, beauty, order, vitality, intelligence, love, of God's perfect Life.

In *Dialogues in Metapsychiatry*, Dr. Hora describes the relation of the good of God to our life-experience:

> If we keep in mind what is really good, everything in our lives will be turning out good. It is important to have the right concept and the right understanding of what the good really is. Our experience in this world is but a shadow of spiritual reality. In order for the shadow to be good, the substance has to be clearly defined. What is the substance of reality? It is the intangible good which is in our consciousness. If the substance is clearly defined in consciousness, it casts a perfect shadow and to us it appears as good experience in daily living.

But we must not be interested in the good of God primarily in the hope that it will pay off in a material way, because we are not then sincere seekers of the truth; we have ulterior motives. But if we are sincerely interested in knowing the real good, then, of course, we will be blessed in every way, even in the material world, because the material world is the shadow of spiritual reality.[2]

Let's rerun the marital movie starring Helen and Jerry, this time with the good of God directing the action. It is Saturday night, and Helen and Jerry have just had their discussion-cum-argument. Helen is furious over what Jerry said. But she doesn't want to go to bed mad, because she knows that it will fester over the night, and she'll be really sunk in ego and misery by morning. So she tells Jerry that she needs to take some time alone, and she goes off to a quiet spot to think and pray. "What am I so mad about?" she asks herself. She immediately replies, "At Jerry, because he's such a rat fink!" And then: "O.K., he's a rat fink. You didn't like what he said. But what are you most interested in? Do you want badness to run this show, cause you a sleepless night, louse up your life together, poison the atmosphere for the baby? If you go with your anger, it is not Jerry who's to blame. You're letting the sea of mental garbage take over. Jerry is not in this world to please you. His ignorance is between him and God. Maybe what he said was garbage, but you have a chance to stop the garbage right now. What are you interested in: garbage or good?"

When we put the good of God first, it means taking the time to examine the issue in the light of spiritual good. The ego always disguises its concerns in such a way that we do not see clearly at first what the real issue is. So we need to be on the lookout for the telltale signs of ego: "I, me,

2. Quote is from page 61 of the *Dialogues*.

mine . . . I want . . . gimme . . ." and the reactions to those concerns: "You're to blame . . . it's your fault . . . you didn't . . . you did. . . ." In marriage, when we are feeling upset with our spouse, we can always cut through the distractions by asking first, "What am I most interested in?" We may not choose the good of God, and there is no "should" about it. We may, if we wish, be more interested in the tempting ego-goodie of the moment. That's O. K. If we have asked ourselves the question of interest, then at least we will be clear that it is our choice, and we will be able to evaluate the consequences of our choice. If we don't like the consequences, we will be motivated to choose differently next time.

Recently the newspaper reported on a ninety-eight-year-old couple who have been married seventy-nine years. The man stated that they had never had a quarrel and gave the following advice: "Don't say nothing when an argument starts. Just turn around and walk off by yourself, saying there ain't nothing to get mad about, that she didn't mean no harm." Now, *that's* being interested in the good. Wouldn't it have been wonderful if Helen and Jerry, at the moment of their hostile reactions, could have, instead, walked off by themselves, saying that there is nothing to get mad about, that he and she didn't mean any harm? With the good of God directing the show, Helen and Jerry's marital movie would have dissolved into nothingness, and the "Sunday morning massacre" would never have taken place.

Mind-Fasting and Spirit-Feasting:
Asking for the Good of God

Giving ourselves the chance to "taste" harmony in situations where we would have previously let ego dominate with discord begins to whet our appetites for the good.

Our old identification with negative experience needs to yield to the recognition that joy, harmony, health, and abundance are possible—even to us. We will be much more likely to give ourselves this opportunity if we follow a regular practice of mentally tasting the good, and this is done by regular prayer, meditation and spiritual study.

The concern underlying any valid form of meditation and prayer is for consciousness to become free from the incessant babbling of ego-dominated thought patterns so that transcendental awareness can break through. Just as you cannot hear anything as long as you are talking, so you cannot be conscious of anything else as long as you are mentally talking to yourself. Just listen to your mental babblings sometime. They are dreadfully tiresome, noisy and repetitious, like a broken record. When people become interested in knowing the good of God, they seek ways to turn off the record player so that, in the stillness of transcendental awareness, they may hear and realize spiritual Reality. Right prayer and meditation and spiritual study are the ways we learn to ask for the good and become receptive to it.

Two forms of meditation which are easily accessible to busy people and which can easily be taught to children are termed "mind-fasting" and "spirit-feasting."[3] Mind-fasting is a term of ancient origin in Eastern, perhaps Taoist, thought. In our usage it refers to a process of "starving" one's old, false views of reality by refraining from pursuing the thoughts which are based upon these views. For example, if I wake up in the morning feeling tired and grouchy, I am tempted to complain about it, nag and holler at the kids, feel sorry for myself because I lead such a burdened existence and go back to bed when the family has left. However, noticing that this approach tends to start everyone off

3. Bernard J. Tyrrell, *Christotherapy* (New York: Seabury Press, 1975), p. 73.

on the wrong foot, since such self-confirmatory indulgence
is very contagious, I might decide instead to mind-fast.
Every time a negative thought came into consciousness, I
would challenge it, seeing it not as my thought but as a
garbage thought and remanding it to the "sea" from
whence it came. Likewise, negative feelings of fatigue and
irritation would be called into question and firmly returned
to their parent ignorance. We cannot prevent garbage
thoughts from coming into consciousness, but we don't
have to believe or hang onto them just because they are
there. In the words of a Chinese motto: "You can't stop the
birds from flying over your head, but you don't need to let
them nest in your hair."

More than mind-fasting is needed, however, for a
receptivity to spiritual good. Mindful of Jesus' parable
about the man who becomes free of one "unclean spirit"
only to have it return with seven more, even "more evil,"[4]
we do not content ourselves with simply mind-fasting. If
the ego is being starved, the real being needs to be nour-
ished, and this is where "spirit-feasting" is important. This
is a practice of filling consciousness with thoughts of spiritual good, cherishing ideas about God's perfect spiritual
Reality. It means loving Love and Life and Beauty and
Goodness and seeking to discern these everywhere. This
can be done by reading certain passages from the Bible or
other spiritual literature which points to these realities, by
noticing the beauty and harmony and loveliness of the
natural world, or by bringing to mind spiritual values even
while one is busy with something else.

In Southern California the abundance and beauty of
divine Love are always visible through the richness of the
vegetation, year round. Having moved here from the heart
of Manhattan, I continue to feel blessed to sit in the yard,

---

4. Luke 11:24-26.

surrounded by green and blooming things all year. I think of a flower as God's Love made visible or remember the words attributed to St. Francis: "I said to the almond tree, 'Speak to me of God.' And the almond tree blossomed."

Some years ago, when our younger boy was a baby, I was tending him in the middle of the night. He seemed to be in pain but there was nothing clearly wrong; he just fussed and fussed and fussed. Feeling helpless and somewhat desperate, I prayed to realize God's presence. A statement which I had read somewhere popped into my mind. It said something like, "The belief of a child in pain reveals a lack of understanding of the nature of divine Love." A sense of ignorance welled up and I said out loud, "Oh, Eriky, we just don't know enough about Love." Eventually he quieted and I went back to bed. The next morning, after putting the boys down for their nap, I suddenly felt an urge to get outside for my meditation time. As I looked around the yard, the green foliage everywhere seemed alive with Love; every growing thing spoke a personal message of Love to me, and the thought kept going through my mind, "You have to be blind not to see this." It was as if some inner screen of "busyness" and preoccupation had dropped, momentarily, and I could see clearly what is real. For that moment, I was totally open to the good of God. The perception passed; I became "blind" again. Yet that moment of spiritual discernment continues to enrich my spirit-feasting, for though the inner veil remains in place, I know that the message of Love is still there.

Although the natural world may facilitate spirit-feasting, city-dwellers need not despair. Spirit knows no urban blight. Seeing beyond the masks of personhood to the "child of God" in other people is a very challenging and potent form of spirit-feasting. When the little children in our neighborhood were occasionally scared by a somewhat disturbed teenage boy recently, I found myself feeling a bit apprehensive every time I saw him walking on our street. He dressed himself to look as fierce as possible, complete with black leather clothes, black boots and "shades," and he liked to say frightening things to the children as he passed. One day, when I saw him walking by and felt my usual revulsion, a text I had read recently came to mind. The verse says, "Thine eyes shall see the king in his beauty; they shall behold the land that is very far off" (Isaiah 33:17). Looking at the boy, I suddenly thought, "No, not a disturbed teenager, but 'the king in his beauty.'" Every time thereafter that I saw him, I would think, "The king in his beauty." Spiritual good is always there, wherever you are looking, behind the masks of evil which ignorance creates. Being interested in good means preferring to focus on the secret beauty of spirit rather than on the ugliness of ego's self-promotional displays.

It may be hardest for us to mind-fast and spirit-feast in connection with our spouses and other family members, but it is therefore most important that we do so, for we are most ego-involved with those people. If we are interested in the good of God, we will be interested in the good of our husbands, wives and children and will regularly remind ourselves of it. In the family setting, it is supremely easy for our attention to get hooked on the negatives of behavior—what the other person does that I don't like—and to take for granted the spiritual qualities which manifest themselves.

One young wife laughingly recalled that one of the reasons she married her husband was that he was so generous toward others. However, after they married, his continued generosity of himself and his time toward other people began to bug her. He was supposed to be generous toward her, not toward every Tom, Dick and Harry. But she could see and laugh at her own possessiveness, and then continue to appreciate his good qualities.

We need to take regular periods of time away from distractions for prayer, meditation and spiritual study. But more than that, we need to be interested in thinking about the good of God, moment by moment, if we would build up our receptivity to spiritual Reality. Your eyes "shall behold the land that is very far off" only as your interest in and love for that land—the domain of Spirit—outweighs your love for the old, familiar landscape of the ego.

SUMMARY

"Thou shalt have no other interests before the Good of God, which is spiritual" (Principle 1 of the Metapsychiatry).

• The good of God means the spiritual qualities which enhance life and promote health. All the activities and forms of our experience require spiritual good—love, intelligence, beauty, harmony, freedom, peace, joy—if they are to be valuable.

• The ego has no reliable standard for what is good: it judges "good" whatever confirms itself. Ego-judgment therefore often calls the good "bad" and the bad "good."

• Interest may take three forms: cherishing, hating and fearing. All three involve mental preoccupation which keeps us involved with what we are interested in. To become free from something we must lose interest in it.

• The only way to lose interest in ego-good is to become more interested in the good of God. Mind-fasting and spirit-feasting are daily disciplines for promoting our receptivity to spiritual good.

4. People
Are Not Porcupines

"There is no interaction anywhere: there is only Omniaction everywhere" (Principle 3 of Metapsychiatry).

Principle 3 is such a radical statement that we cannot hope or expect simply to understand it: "Oh, yes, I see . . . how interesting." It is a genuine koan: a statement which does not fit in with ordinary intellectual reasoning but which is designed precisely to shatter our basic concepts of reality. It is a wonderful statement to meditate upon, for it leads consciousness into transcendental realms.

Nonetheless, the principle can be extremely valuable as a guide and pointer to Reality for anyone who takes it seriously, no matter what that individual's level of realization. When it comes to marriage, the principle gets to the very heart of the matter in the most incisive way. Marriage, in its popular definition, is nothing but interaction—interpersonal interaction. If there is no interaction anywhere, what happens to marriage?

If we would understand the practical implications of Principle 3 for marriage, we must first ask, "What is interaction?" The dictionary defines it as "action on each other; reciprocal action or effect." Interaction is the belief that separate entities act upon one another, cause effects upon each other. Interpersonal interaction applies the term to people, seeing each individual as a separate center of action, with the centers doing things to, and being done unto by, others. There is an implicit belief that each center of action has some sort of power—power to act upon others and, perhaps, to resist being acted upon.

In view of the discussion in Chapter 2 of the nature of the ego-perspective as that of a "goose in a bottle," it is clear that the idea of interaction between people presupposes that perspective. The term "interpersonal interaction" makes the underlying view of reality very explicit. The word "person" comes from the Latin term "persona" meaning "mask." It points up, then, the essentially fictitious nature of an individual's ego, or ideas about himself. And when you consider the emphasis in our culture on personhood—having respect for persons, treating another as a person, concern with being treated by others as a person, etc.—the problem is exposed. Individuals identify with a counterfeit self and then proceed to defend and promote it at all costs.

Well, what's so wrong with thinking of yourself as a person and wanting to be treated like one? Let's take a look at how this thinking operates in our views of marriage and relationships, so that we can better understand its troublesome consequences.

The focus on interpersonal interaction began with the influence of Harry Stack Sullivan in the field of psychiatry. He made a strong case for the importance that interactions with "significant" persons have on the development of the ego, for good or ill, throughout our lives. In various forms, this belief in the power of interpersonal interactions to determine our health and happiness continues to be a strong influence in psychological thinking. In Transactional Analysis, one of the most popular forms of psychological treatment today, it shows up described as "strokes," i.e., interpersonal affirmations, which are considered absolutely essential to human development and well being.

Taken over into popular thinking, these ideas form the basis for a preoccupation with relationships. Almost everyone would agree nowadays that relationships are the most important thing in life, and that it is impossible for humans to be human without constructive relationships throughout their lives. We believe that we have a basic, human need for the attention and affirmation of our fellow humans, and there is, in our culture, a universal orgy of questing after the interpersonal "produce" which we believe we need. Singles either seek permanent relationships or a "swinging" life of numerous interactions with numerous persons; married folk calculate and manipulate to get their "needs" met by their partners, and parents and children of all ages continue to blame and/or emotionally blackmail one another in an on-going search for the "right" interpersonal interactions.

One mother, whose grown daughter had been in various psychotherapies for years, told me of her dismay when the girl, paying one of her rare-and-hostile visits to her mother, suddenly screamed out, "You never would let me have a black dress, and I always wanted one." (No wonder TV commercials picture a harried woman asking, "What's a mother to do?")

This particular incident demonstrates the painful and self-defeating consequences of a belief in interpersonal interaction. It is so difficult to manage the flow of produce to and from others satisfactorily. You never get as much as you want of what you think you need from others, and what you provide to others is never adequate by their—or your own—standards. And it's an endless hassle. Trying to get your personal needs met while meeting other people's personal needs, plus defending yourself against the "bad" produce from others and managing your own reactions so that you don't dump too much "bad" produce on them . . . whew! It keeps a person busy mentally—and causes stress. The word "cope" is a slogan of our times. I would estimate that virtually all of the plethora of self-help workshops offered across the country deal with ways of coping with others or with yourself. I recently chuckled over a flyer advertising a workshop on "stress skills." The final topic offered "101 specific ways of coping with stress." We are not only subjected to stress because of our coping, but we then must cope with our stress—in 101 ways, yet.

People who "need people" are not lucky; they are porcupines. That is the image someone has used to describe the human condition in our times: porcupines who must huddle close enough together to stay warm, yet stay far enough apart not to poke each other too severely. It is a tentative and uncomfortable situation at best, unbearable at worst. And it is in marriage that it is most likely to become unbearable. Given the belief in the importance of interpersonal produce, marriage tends to be motivated by the desire to secure the right produce for oneself, to guarantee that one's needs get met over the long haul. Yet that very belief puts an unbearable weight on the marriage partnership. The belief that our well-being lies in the hands of one other person makes a god out of that person—a false god who usually then turns into a devil. There is nothing mysterious about the fact that the majority of murders are committed against family members, people's so-called "loved ones." The belief in interpersonal interaction makes one feel both needy and vulnerable, and those are very painful feelings. When a person's "loved one" fails to properly relieve the pain, the disappointment and blame are severe.

The depth of bitterness between many couples who come for counseling is still stunning to me. Here are people who reportedly loved one another enough at one time to commit themselves to sharing life together. Yet, by the time they seek help, they are completely unable even to entertain a kindly thought toward each other. Each is so furiously blaming the other for his or her pain that the idea of trying to help one another is unthinkable to them.

The remarkable degree of hostility between marriage partners reveals the importance of the basic issue involved. If a casual acquaintance or co-worker fails to live up to an expectation in some way, an individual does not become distraught. It is when one looks to another to supply his or her basic life needs and is disappointed that feelings of hurt and rage and blame can become murderous. But the intensity of feeling exposes the falsity of the expectations. To expect another human to provide one with security, peace, love, self-esteem, and happiness is unrealistic. It is like expecting to get sunshine from others. They cannot provide it; it is not theirs to give. It is the expectation which is at fault, not the people.

Now, perhaps, it is possible to see what is wrong with thinking of ourselves as interacting persons. It makes us feel lousy and leads us to pour our energy into self-defeating and sometimes destructive endeavors. Worst of all, it completely blinds us to Omniaction, wherein, alone, we can find the relief from fear, the healing for our pain, and the constructive avenues of living for which we long.

"There is no interaction anywhere; there is only Omniaction everywhere." Omniaction: catch even a glimpse of what it means, and unprecedented freedom and joy are yours. "Omni-" means "all, everywhere." Omniaction refers to a single Source of all action, a single Power, manifesting itself in all being and activity. Principle 3, then, declares that instead of an infinite number of separate entities acting upon one another in unpredictable and often chaotic ways, Life actually consists of the eternal, harmonious activity of God, Omniactive Love-Intelligence, expressing itself everywhere, in an infinite variety of ways.

In the light of Omniaction, our definition of man is

necessarily radically altered. The idea of man as an autono-mous, skin-encapsulated ego is shattered. Man is found to be a manifestation of God's Life and activity, one with his divine Source, as the sunbeam is one with the sun or the wave one with the ocean. Man is a spiritual consciousness through which the good of God flows into form and ex-pression in all areas of life. As Eric Butterworth says, "We are all in the express business."[1] We are not consumers of life; we are manifestations of Life.

For many people, the idea of Omniaction seems to make us more separate than ever, without even the prickly-but-comforting attempt to get close to others. If we are all individual expressions of Omniactive Love-Intelligence, and if life is a matter of learning how to let spiritual realities flow through consciousness into the world, it sounds pretty lonely. What connection is there between me and somebody else? If I don't need other people and they don't need me, then don't we all become like hermits, living in little solitary caves out in the desert, just sitting and meditating? Certainly, there doesn't seem to be any signifi-cance to marriage.

In this sort of reaction to the idea of Omniaction we can see the extent to which the belief in interpersonal needs governs our thinking. The term "need" has become almost synonymous with the word "love"; we can't imagine what love could be without the sense of mutual need. A current TV commercial for an insurance company pictures a mother and a father delightedly affirming with regard to their spouses and children: "They need me." The delight implies a further, unspoken belief: "They need me . . . therefore I must be valuable, important, loved."

1. See Eric Butterworth, *Discover the Power Within You* (New York: Harper and Row, 1968).

Omniaction, though it destroys the belief in interpersonal interaction as a source of existential—basic life—supply, does not destroy the individuality or worth of the individual, nor the value of shared human experience. Strangely enough, it elevates the quality and worth of both individuality and togetherness. To use a simple analogy, it is something like swimmers in a pool. If an individual is to develop his own potential as a swimmer, and if he is also to enjoy participating with others in the pool in a constructive way, he must first learn how to cooperate with the buoyancy so that he may float. Someone who thinks others should hold him up remains inhibited in developing his own capacities and becomes a nuisance, perhaps even a hazard, to the other swimmers.

Omniaction is the buoyancy of Life. Life will float us, support us, even guide and protect and bloom us, when we learn how to cooperate with it so that we can allow that to happen. But obviously, if we are clinging to the edge of a pool in a panic, or grabbing onto and wrestling with others, we won't be able to learn a thing about floating. When our minds are full of interaction thinking, something like that is going on, and we won't be receptive to the understanding of Omniaction.

The principle of Omniaction tells us that our existential needs are met by God and not by other people. It tells us something that we can never, never discover as long as we live in the realm of interpersonal interaction: it tells us that Life is basically good and benevolent and that God is Love. Life, in Interactionsville, is just what the old saying declares: "One (blasted) thing after another!" Life in Omniaction is pure bliss, as witnessed to in the following descriptions:

And the Lord will guide you continually,
and satisfy your desire with good things,

and make your bones strong;
and you shall be like a watered garden
(Isaiah 58:11).

It is interesting to compare this biblical poetry with the words of a woman who became enlightened through the Zen meditation discipline:

> I feel a consciousness which is neither myself nor not myself, which is protecting or leading me into directions helpful to my proper growth and maturity, and propelling me away from that which is against that growth. It is like a stream into which I have flowed and, joyously, is carrying me beyond myself.[2]

Jesus taught:

> Do not be anxious about your life, what you shall eat, nor about your body, what you shall put on. For life is more than food and the body more than clothing. Consider the ravens: they neither sow nor reap, they have neither storehouse nor barn, and yet God feeds them. Of how much more value are you than the birds!

> And which of you by being anxious can add a cubit to his span of life? If then you are not able to do as small a thing as that, why are you anxious about the rest? Consider the lilies, how they grow; they neither toil nor spin; yet I tell you, even Solomon in all his glory was not arrayed like one of these. But if God so clothes the grass which is alive in the field today and tomorrow is thrown

2. Philip Kapleau, ed., *The Three Pillars of Zen* (Boston: Beacon Press, 1965), p. 268.

into the oven, how much more will he clothe you,
O men of little faith!

And do not seek what you are to eat and what you
are to drink, nor be of anxious mind. For all the
nations of the world seek these things; and your
Father knows that you need them. Instead, seek
his kingdom and these things shall be yours as
well. Fear not, little flock, for it is your Father's
good pleasure to give you the kingdom (Luke
12:22-32).

Jesus' familiar words are usually considered to be very
beautiful but quite unrealistic. In all of my years as a
church member, seminary student and church professional,
I never met anyone who thought Jesus really meant what
he said, in a down-to-earth, practical sense. But Jesus always meant what he said. He described for us the nature of
Reality; he taught and demonstrated the spiritual laws,
laws which work the same way for us as they did for him,
when we respect them as he respected them. This sermon is
a description of Omniaction. It ends with the suggestion
that if we want our lives to flourish on all levels, we need
to stop trying to manage our affairs—cope with the details—and we need to develop that consciousness of God
which allows Omniaction to operate unimpeded in our
lives. And there is the final reassurance that even that
"task"—the seeking of the kingdom of God—is something
we don't "do" but is a gift from God: "It is the Father's
good pleasure to give you the kingdom."

Omniaction and Love go together; any realization of
either brings a realization of the other. Love, as a principle
of Existence, is not realizable on the level of interpersonal
interaction, because on that level love is both fleeting and
disappointing. We are always disappointing others and
they are always disappointing us. Affairs between persons

are always temporary and flawed, so that the idea of personal love, even if raised to the highest level of a personal God's personal love, lacks the necessary divine attributes of being eternal and unchangeable.

Omniaction is the spiritual law of Love. It says that the only thing which is really at work anywhere and anytime is the activity of perfect Life: being itself, showing itself, knowing itself. We therefore do not have to cope with others, nor do we have to manage ourselves. We need only "lift up our eyes," open our consciousness, to the transpersonal, spiritual realm. When we do that, when we acknowledge that behind the appearances of things and selves and interactions is actually the one Power and Reality, divine Love-Intelligence, then we relax our grip, and problems tend to resolve, and things tend to unfold harmoniously. We yield in consciousness to What Is—Omniaction—in much the same way that we yield, physically, to the "isness" of buoyancy. By the yielding we allow the action of What Is to operate in our experience.

The practicality of this understanding came home (literally, as you will see) to my husband and me when we were negotiating with our landlord for the purchase of the house which we had been renting for several years. Although we had always had a most cordial relationship with the landlord, when it came to buying and selling, we found self-interest rearing its ugly head. In our first discussion, he quoted us a price which we thought was exorbitant, and when we tried to discuss the pros and cons, we all became somewhat defensive. He left, saying that he would return in a week's time and that we should have a counter-proposal ready for him at that time.

In the intervening week, we did our practical home-work, and this was not encouraging, for it appeared that we would not be able to buy the house unless he reduced his price considerably. Yet it seemed important to us to stay in what had become our home, and it seemed existentially valid for us to expect that this would be possible. We decided to apply, as best we could, the spiritual principles which are the foundation of our home life to this seeming problem.

It was clear that if we stayed on the mental level of interpersonal interaction, we had a lot to lose. If we got defensive or angry, which was easy to do on that level, it would only harden the landlord's position. Every time I was tempted to argue the case with him mentally (which was frequently), I instead acknowledged that there were not several separate, conflicting egos, but rather the one Omniactive divine Mind, unfolding intelligence and goodness to all. It appeared that either he must "lose" or we must "lose," but I consistently affirmed that in Omniaction, everyone always wins. The unfoldment of good anywhere is a blessing everywhere.

When the landlord returned the following week, we were much in suspense, but ready to stand firm in the principle of Omniaction. Before we could say a word, he informed us that a whole new plan had occurred to him during the week, which seemed to meet everybody's needs. He proceeded to unfold a plan which did, indeed, meet all our needs, enabling us to buy the house and save several thousand dollars which we divided with him, so that he was also blessed by the transaction. We were speechless. We could never have figured out the plan he offered. We closed the deal immediately in a state of great harmony and goodness for everybody involved.

Coping with other people is dangerous. It brings out their "quills." The more we acknowledge that there is a higher Power and Intelligence in operation, the freer our lives become from stress and friction.

It may be hardest to understand what Omniaction means in relation to marriage. Since we believe marriage to be made up totally of interpersonal interaction, when we turn our attention to Omniaction it seems that marriage disappears altogether. What is a marriage without interaction? It is just what it has been defined to be: a joint participation in the good of God, a spiritual partnership. The image of ballroom dancers is useful in getting an idea of what is involved:

> Anyone who would attempt to dance without music would certainly appear to be moving about in a very clumsy and graceless way. Such an individual would be imposing certain willful ideas on himself concerning how to move.

> If two people attempted to dance together without music, they would be interacting with each other in a more or less willful and discordant way. They might cooperate or resist each other intermittently. In any case, it would be a difficult situation.

> It is clear, then, that dancing is neither personal action nor interpersonal action. Dancing is responding, yielding, obeying the promptness of music. A good dancer allows himself to be controlled by the music. Right dancing is joint participation in the rhythmic action of music.

> Dance is a helpful analogy illustrating the third principle. Omniaction is the *soundless music of existence*, and we must learn to be governed by it or else our life-experiences will be discordant.[3]

---

3. From *The Soundless Music of Life*, an unpublished teaching paper by Thomas Hora, M.D.

Marriage does not disappear in Omniaction; it is trans-formed. The push-and-pull is gone, the jerkiness, the stepped-on toes. When the focus is on the music, marriage is neither essential nor impossible. One can dance alone without it being a deprivation, so the situation of the unmarried individual loses its supposed poignancy. But one may dance with another, and it carries with it a special joy and enrichment. The love of the joint participation is moti-vating—one wants to be attentive to the music and respond well for the joy of the harmonious movement together; the requirement of joint participation is disciplining—one be-comes immediately aware of a disharmonious movement—and the sharing of joint participation is potentiating—the better my partner dances, the better I dance; the better I dance, the better my partner dances.

Human beings are not porcupines—and they are not parasites. No human being can authentically govern his or her affairs by the wishes or demands of another. Love cannot be commanded. Respect for, reverence for, the in-tegrity of another individual are absolutely essential for wholesome togetherness. The belief in interpersonal need always undermines and sabotages the love and respect we would like to hold for others.

For example, when Ellen returned home from a week of visiting relatives, Fred, her husband of nearly thirty years, told her that he had to go to the hospital while she was gone. Feeling very ill late one evening, he had become alarmed and had called a young woman who worked for him, with whom he was quite friendly, to ask if she would take him to the hospital. Upon hearing that Fred had called that young woman for aid, Ellen became hysterical, declar-ing that he didn't love her or he would not have called that woman whom he knew Ellen was jealous of, etc., etc. There was not one word, not one thought given to Fred's need, the seriousness of his condition, or the anxiety of being alone and ill in the night. Ellen hadn't a crumb to offer her husband of many years. She was completely captive to her own sense of need and her rage at having her insecurity triggered by Fred's mention of his feminine employee.

We want to be loving to our loved ones, but a sense of interpersonal need keeps us calculating and manipulating to get the needs met. Far from being synonymous, "need" and "love" are mutually exclusive, for, says Dr. Hora in a surprising statement, "The opposite of love is not hate, as is generally assumed. The opposite of love is calculative thinking."[4] Calculating to get our needs met, we turn our loved ones into objects for our use, and marriage becomes what one marriage counselor described it to be: "mutual exploitation."

But Omniaction facilitates our best intentions. Freed from the belief that we have to get what we need from other people, we take our needs and problems to God and find an increasing sense of the buoyancy of life in all our concerns. We begin to understand what it means to say that God is Love, and we also begin to be able to demonstrate that Love, which is, actually, the only love that is love.

Abraham Maslow, a rare psychologist who concerned himself with the study of health rather than pathology, makes the following comments about what he describes as "B-love" which is "unneeding love, love for the Being of another person."

B-love is welcomed into consciousness and is completely enjoyed. Since it is non-possessive, and is admiring rather than needing, it makes no trouble. . . .

4. Thomas Hora, *In Quest of Wholeness* (Garden Grove: Christian Counseling Service, 1972), p. 141.

It can never be sated; it may be enjoyed without
end. It usually grows greater rather than disap-
pearing. It is end rather than means.

In B-love there is a minimum of anxiety-hostility.
For all practical human purposes, it may even be
considered to be absent.

B-lovers are more independent of each other, less
jealous or threatened, less needful, more individual, more disinterested, but also simultaneously
more eager to help the other toward self-actual-
ization, more proud of his triumphs, more altruis-
tic, generous and fostering.[5]

We don't need to be afraid that letting go of interaction thinking means losing valuable relationships; quite the
contrary, it means freeing those relationships to become a
joint participation in the good of God, within which the
partners become true lovers, helping and sharing with one
another in an atmosphere of benevolence.

Most of us are not yet on the level of B-love, but a
commitment to Omniaction helps to bring us there. Whenever we choose to act on the basis of a desire to express
spiritual values rather than on the basis of trying to make
something happen interpersonally, we have fostered our
capacity for true love.

For example, Gene and Karla had been painting their
study. Most of the bookcases and furniture had been put
back, but a large vase, which went on top of the bookcase,
had not been put back. Because Gene could reach it with-

5. Abraham Maslow, *Toward a Psychology of Being* (Princeton: D. van Nostrand Co.,
   Inc., 1962), p. 40.

out having to get a stepladder, Karla had asked him to put it back. He agreed, but forgot to do it. She began to nag him about it and he, predictably, kept putting it off. One Saturday when Karla walked in the door to find Gene sitting in a chair reading and the vase still on the kitchen counter, she lost her cool and screamed, "Will you put that thing back where it belongs?"

Gene, at this point, had a choice: he could go with interaction or he could go with Omniaction. The ego-voice said, "She's dumped some bad produce on you by screaming at you. Don't take it lying down. Give her some garbage back." So he was strongly tempted to shout back at her and march in a huff from the room. That choice offered a lot of self-confirmatory goodies. He could feel self-righteous and abused for probably the whole weekend, and he could use her "bad produce" as an excuse for being obnoxious himself. However, there would also be a lot of negative fallout, he knew from experience. Karla would also sulk and brood the whole weekend, and they would both take it out on the kids, who would turn grumpy and tearful and fight all the time. And he'd go to work on Monday in a vile mood that would louse up the whole day. So much for interaction. No love there.

Or he could go with Omniaction. Recognizing that "there is no interaction anywhere"—nothing real had taken place between them in her outburst, and he was not "damaged" in any way—he could remind himself that he didn't need to "handle" Karla in any way. If he stayed out of the way, she could have the opportunity to see for herself the inappropriateness of her screaming. Pausing a moment to ask himself "What is *my* issue here?" it would become immediately obvious to him that the intelligent and loving response would be to put the vase where it belonged. If he did that graciously, out of a recognition that his prior resistance to putting it back—again, interaction thinking—

had tended to provoke the unpleasantness, the situation would be healed. The whole family could enjoy a pleasant weekend, and everyone could head out Monday morning, fresh and peaceful, with their minds alert and free from interpersonal garbage. Omniaction is the home of Love.

It needs to be clarified, however, that saying that there is no interaction and working to resolve family frictions through that understanding does not mean that we must tolerate and live with destructive behavior. A clear perception of divine Reality gives us a clear sense of what is wholesome and what is not. And we do not encourage, in ourselves or others, unhealthy self-indulgence. We cannot tell another, not even a husband or wife, what he or she has to do or be. But we must be clear about our own values and not settle for a quality of life which is lacking. Sometimes an individual simply has to say, "I can't live with this, or I can't permit the children to live with this. If you choose to continue in this path, you are choosing to end the marriage."

However, separation and divorce are such easy and popular "outs" these days that I hesitate even to mention them. The real issue here is the realization that interaction thinking produces and supports marital friction and problems. In a marriage, unhealthy behavior on the part of a spouse is usually supported by the thoughts and behavior of the other partner. As we say, "It takes two to tango." When one partner pulls out of the sick setup between them, by pulling out of interaction thinking, it usually resolves the problem. Either the spouse leaves the marriage in search of someone else with whom to continue the unhealthy game, or that individual begins to be freed from the desire to indulge in it, since it no longer "works" on an interaction level. Identifying the real culprit, interaction thinking, is crucial to our well being. For, even if a couple separate, as long as they stay on the level of interaction thinking, seeking their well-being in the offerings of another person, their troubles will recur, with each other and/or new "porcupines."

Many people, when first introduced to these ideas, acknowledge that they represent the most constructive way of understanding and responding to things but think that it is quite impossible for them to behave in such a way. "When in the grip of strong feelings," they ask, "how do you make yourself not react?"

The answer is that you don't have to make yourself do or not do anything. If you are interested in improving the quality of your life, then you will grow in understanding, and it is understanding that "does" what needs to be done.

It might be helpful to understand what it is about interaction thinking and the feelings that go along with it which are so captivating. Interaction is captivating to the extent that you believe that it constitutes Reality. If what goes on between people is *it*, the ultimate realm of life, the place where you either get, or fail to get, your life fulfilled, then what happens there *matters*. And if it *matters*, then you can't simply drop it as if it didn't matter.

Omniaction is the absolute liberator of human consciousness from interaction thinking, because it tells us what we need to know. It tells us that what happens in interaction does not matter very much, *because it is not Real*. It is a "friction of fictions," a dream. When you are dreaming that you are being chased by a fearsome monster, you feel as if your life were in danger; it is of utmost importance that you escape. When you awake and realize that it was a dream, you feel instantly relieved, and there is no inclination to continue searching for a means of escape. Your awakening was the escape; you are free.

Any little glimpse of Omniaction, any small willingness to acknowledge God's allness, helps free us from the tyranny of interaction thinking. Any freedom from interaction thinking frees us automatically from the problems associated therewith. Just as awakening from the dream frees you from not only the belief in the awful chase, but also from the terror and helplessness, the pounding heart and sweating palms associated with that belief, so awakening from the dream of interaction frees you from the physical, emotional and behavioral aspects of that dream. Because overall stress is gradually reduced as we grow in an understanding of Omniaction, stress-managing behaviors such as smoking, drinking, drug use, compulsive eating and talking, etc., tend to resolve.

A belief in personhood will try to convince you that it is important to cling to the idea that interaction matters: that if it doesn't matter what others have "done" to you, then that amounts to saying that you don't count, you are not important. "So," whispers ye olde ego, "hang onto your anger, your blame, your hurt. It matters."

Omniaction says, "It matters that you know who you really are and where your fulfillment really lies. Personal sense will rob you of the peace, joy and abundance which are your birthright as a child of God. You are 'The king's (son or) daughter . . . all glorious within: (your) clothing is of wrought gold' (Psalm 45:13). Your life is a manifestation of the good of God. It is therefore not only your existential privilege but your existential duty to demonstrate health, goodness, beauty, abundance and joy." (Would you really rather be a porcupine?)

Two practical ways of keeping out of the snare of interpersonal thinking might be called basic tools of transpersonal concern. First of all, when there seems to be a problem of interaction with someone, always ask yourself, "What, in my thinking and my behavior may be contributing to this difficulty?" When your attention is on the issue of what you need to learn, you are not feeding into the problem from your side, and that facilitates the working of

Omniaction. Secondly, make a regular practice of seeing yourself and others as individual expressions of Omniaction rather than as personalities.

A very constructive practice in the home is to write "love letters" occasionally to your husband or wife, your children or parents, and especially any family member with whom there seems to be friction. This is no ordinary love letter, of the "I love you" kind, or in the grosser terms recommended by some, "I crave your body." Rather this is a true love letter, because love is concerned to see the good. So it is helpful to sit down, in a moment of quiet, and bring to mind the positive qualities of your spouse or other family member, and write these down in some form. And then, over the next few days, attempt to keep these good qualities foremost in your mind, even, if appropriate, sharing with that individual your appreciation of them.

One word of appreciation, as we all know, is worth more than a thousand naggings or criticisms. When your husband remembers to take out the trash, say, "Thanks," or "It's really nice to have such a reliable husband." Say it even though that is one of his regular tasks. Don't take positive participation for granted. And when your wife, as usual, has a good and hot meal on the table at the right time, let her know that you appreciate it. And when your child does something right, notice it.

Seeing the good, we become facilitators of it, channels for it, instruments of Omniactive Love-Intelligence instead of huddled porcupines. Attentive to the "soundless music of existence" we move with grace and harmony and love, freed from the crippling concern to cope with what's wrong and grab onto what's right.

"As for me, I will behold thy face in righteousness: I shall be satisfied, when I awake, with thy likeness" (Psalm 17:15).

SUMMARY

"There is no interaction anywhere; there is only Omniaction everywhere" (Principle 3 of Metapsychiatry).

• People are not porcupines, struggling for both enough closeness and enough distance from one another to survive. People are channels for the activity of God.

• Don't look to your spouse to supply you with what you need to be healthy, happy, fulfilled. Your needs are met in your own consciousness, by divine Love-Intelligence.

• Your spouse's well-being is not up to you; you don't have to rescue, remodel or run him or her. You can be most helpful by simply floating on the buoyancy of Omniaction yourself.

• Love is not related to interpersonal need, which is actually the saboteur of love. Where person is, and where interpersonal interaction is, love is absent.

• Marriage in interaction thinking is like two people trying to dance together without music, pushing and pulling each other on the basis of their ideas about how they should dance.

• Marriage in Omniaction is like ballroom dancers totally attuned to the music, moving in perfect harmony with it and therefore with each other.

• Omniaction is "the soundless music of life."

5. Your Marriage Is None of Your Business

"Take no thought for what should be or what should not be; seek ye first to know the good of God, which already is" (Principle 2 of Metapsychiatry).

In metapsychiatry, Principle 2 is called "the principle of harmonious living." It presents us with two concepts, the understanding of which constitutes the key to harmonious life: "shouldlessness" and "isness."

Like Principle 1, this is a paraphrase of a biblical statement—in this case, Jesus' teaching at the end of the sermon quoted in the last chapter. Jesus says, "And do not seek what you are to eat and what you are to drink, nor be of anxious mind. . . . Instead seek God's kingdom, and these things shall be yours as well" (Luke 12:29-31). The paraphrase, again, helps make contemporary and understandable this extremely significant teaching.

In writing this chapter, I consistently tried to follow my natural inclination to discuss, first, the ordinary level of thinking, should-thinking, and then turn to the existential, spiritual level. And I found that this does not work. When I start out on the level of should-thinking, I get stuck there, and my thinking and writing get more and more complex and confused. From this I have learned not simply a literary, but an existential, lesson. Only from the vantage point of Reality can we see clearly and think intelligently. "In thy light do we see light" (Psalm 36:9). It is a demonstration of Principle 2 that in order to understand it, we need to "seek first" to understand "what is."

The principle states that "what is" is the "good of God." "The good of God ... *already* is." The "already" makes a crucial point. It removes both time and personal effort from the picture. The good of God is not going to come about at some time in the future; it is not a consequence of some action which we, or others, or even God himself, will take. It is—it already is.

> Ho, everyone who thirsts,
> 　　come to the waters;
> and he who has no money,
> 　　come, buy and eat!
> Come, buy wine and milk
> 　　without money and without price.
> (Isaiah 55:1)

The good of God, we have said, is spiritual. The principle is stating that, at every given moment, perfect, spiritual Reality is, and it is the truth of things. It is not an abstract or "ideal" (as popularly contrasted with "real") truth. It is the actual, present substance of every individual's Reality. Everything is already all right, for you and me and everybody else.

This is not to say that everything is already all right in our personal experience, or in the compound personal experience of world affairs. This is what many people find difficult to understand about "isness." They say, "How can you say everything is already all right when I am sick or my husband is unemployed or my child has a birth defect or there is war in the Middle East?" To say that the "good of God already is" is not saying that the "good of personal experience already is." What is going on in our experience is the expression, the taking form, of the thoughts which dominate our consciousness. This is as true for the world-wide, pooled human consciousness as it is for individual consciousness. The fact that we live in a sea of mental garbage is precisely demonstrated by the relentless suffering on all levels of human experience. That suffering exposes the invalidity of the beliefs and thoughts which dominate human consciousness.

Therefore the "bad" of human experience in no way contradicts or calls into question the assertion that "the good of God already is." Rather, it points us in the right direction for the discovery of good. It points "up" instead of "ahead." To find the good, we do not stay on the experience level and look to the future to change things: "Now things are not O. K., but then—when and if such-and-such happens, then things will become good." To find the good we go now, in consciousness, to a different dimension of existence—to the existential-spiritual dimension instead of the personal-experiential dimension—and there we find that things are not as they appeared to be, on the lower level of perception. We find the Reality of all things, and find it to be spiritual and good. And it is that finding, on that level, by way of consciousness, which takes form as the resolution of problems and the unfoldment of good in our experience. "It is our ignorance of God, the divine Principle, which produces apparent discord, and the right understanding of him restores harmony."[1]

The good, then, is never a product of our calculations or manipulations of ourselves, others, our environment or situation. Changes are most harmonious when they occur

---

1. Mary Baker Eddy, *Science and Health with Key to the Scriptures* (Boston: Christian Science Publishing Society), 9 p. 390.

as an unfoldment and expression of a realization in consciousness of the already-actual good. When we act or react out of a sense of the badness of a situation, in an attempt to make things better, we often "jump out of the frying pan into the fire." (How existentially apt these familiar proverbs can be!)

For example, a woman who came with her third husband for marriage counseling confided to the counselor, "Actually, I can now see that my second husband wasn't so bad. If I had known then what I know now, I would have stayed with him, instead of marrying this guy." Trying to make the good happen out of our sense of what is wrong proves to be a very inefficient, not to say fruitless, endeavor. It doesn't work well because, like all such endeavors, it is based on a mistaken idea about the nature of Reality.

On the level of ordinary experience and consciousness, everything appears to be material, changing, limited and imperfect. Autonomous man, the man of this birth-to-death world, is always working to change the appearances in the way he chooses, to make things "better" for himself. He jogs or diets to improve his body, studies to improve his mind, works to improve human conditions or design more efficient technology, strikes or demonstrates for better wages so that his kids can have a better life. And if he isn't working to change things for the better, he lives in the belief that he "should" or that other people "should."

It is the nature of this level of existence, however, that things are always temporary, limited and imperfect. Man can never make himself or his life whole, perfect. Existence in this realm is always dualistic: good and bad. This is where the pinch is felt, described so eloquently by Paul in Romans, "For I do not do the good I want, but the evil I do not want is what I do . . . wretched man that I am" (Romans 7:19, 24). Efforts of persons to help or change other persons have a degrading effect; efforts of persons to improve or change themselves tend to become compulsive and frustrating.

For example, a man, bereft as a boy of wholesome family life, set about to provide himself with an ideal family, marrying a lovely girl and having two children. Twenty-five years later, his wife is divorcing him, his son is rebellious and his daughter had to drop out of college because of depression and anxiety. When he comes for counseling, he can only ask what to do to make his wife stay, and he leaves in despair when he realizes the answer is "nothing." His daughter, stricken with guilt because of her inability to feel comfortable talking with her dad, says, "We were supposed to be his good family, to make up for the one he didn't have when he was a child." We cannot manufacture good lives for ourselves. The goodness, the wholeness, of our lives is something to be discovered, not something to be manufactured.

Only what *is*, already, can ever be. The Real is; the unreal only seems to be. You will never be able to make the Real happen by struggling with what seems to be. You either see Reality now, or you do not. But if you do not, don't bother trying to make it come about. Messing around in the sea of mental garbage will never yield the good, for the good is Real and the sea of mental garbage is not. The good comes into our experience only as the fruit of our conscious realization that it already is.

A spiritual seeker is, by definition, someone who seeks the realization of this higher level of consciousness—spiritual consciousness—in the acknowledgment that that is where real life, real good are to be found. Today, more than ever before, people are realizing that consciousness is the preeminent issue for living, and they are praying and meditating and following various paths in the quest for "enlightenment" or "peace of mind" or "closer relationship with God" or whatever spiritual consciousness is called in that particular tradition.

Whenever anything becomes widely popular, however, it becomes adulterated in various ways. The superficiality and faddiness of much popular concern with Eastern paths, especially Zen and yoga, are obvious, as is "bumper-sticker" Christianity, which demonstrates a singular capacity to trivialize the ineffable. However, perhaps more subtle is the intrusion of the "scientific-autonomous" thinking into the concern with consciousness. Bio-feedback and many forms of meditation developed and promoted in medical or sociological circles have essentially no transcendental referent. They recognize the dominion of the mind over the affairs of the body but remain on the level of personal mind or consciousness. It is still autonomous man attempting—now through various mental techniques—to control himself and his life.

Genuine good is the good of God, it is spiritual Reality, and it already is. It is therefore something to be realized, not created. We arrive, then, back at the thesis of this book, which is that the good which is needed to heal our marriages and family lives necessitates that we become spiritual seekers. People who try to find real healing of interpersonal problems on any level other than the spiritual find, at best, temporary adjustments. The good which they seek is simply not available anywhere except in the spiritual realm.

In light of this understanding of good, we find it much easier to understand the nature of should-thinking and the problems inherent in it. Should-thinking, though condemned in psychological circles as a matter of left-over parental injunctions, involves, existentially, a profound and basic issue. It represents a view of reality which stands in opposition to "isness." Should-thinking reveals the belief that things are not right as they are. It is the universal thought-pattern stemming from ego-consciousness, and it permeates and controls our experiences to a remarkable degree.

We fool ourselves that "shoulds" are guides for constructive behavior. After all, if we don't tell our kids what they should do, how will they know what they should do? And if we don't tell ourselves what we should do, won't we just sink into passivity, settling for the status quo, or drift along with no direction?

Careful observation of one's thoughts, however, reveals that should-thoughts are not related to constructive, responsive behavior. A "should" is not really a guide, it is a negative judgment, and negative judgments are discouraging, not facilitating. If I say to our boys, "Let's see how clean you can get your room in twenty minutes," I clearly expect them to clean it up and believe that they can do it, and the task may get done. But if I say to them, "You boys should clean up your room," I have said not only, "Your room is dirty," but also "You are not doing anything about it, and that is bad." Rather than stimulating them to action, this will probably make them feel resentful and discouraged, and the room will stay uncleaned.

Should-thinking, then, not only expresses the belief that things are not O. K. but is coupled with a sense of personal condemnation, either of self or others, that this is the case. Obviously, it is not a constructive pattern of thought. Yet anyone who takes the time to consistently observe his mental life will find that it is simply saturated with should-thinking. The shoulds may not be directly stated, but they are part of every preconceived idea we have about everything, and they underlie every judgment we make, all day long, about everything under the sun. They also underlie every emotional upset. An emotional upset is the emotional counterpart of the thought that something either should be and isn't or should not be and is.

For example, one woman became upset when her husband failed to kiss her regularly going and coming to and from work. She thought she was upset because of his behavior, but she was really upset because she cherished the thought: "He should kiss me every time he leaves and comes home." Another woman became upset because her husband did kiss her regularly when leaving and coming home. She thought she was upset because of his behavior, but she was really upset because she cherished the thought, "If he kisses me regularly, it becomes automatic and meaningless; therefore he should not kiss me regularly."

Another aspect of should-thinking is revealed by these examples, and that is that should-thinking is personally-willful thinking. I am making judgments based upon my personal opinions about everything, thereby presuming that I both can and have the right to impose my will upon Reality.

Should-thinking is the tool of self-confirmation; it proclaims, "Reality should conform to my particular views, terms, desires." We cling to our "shoulds" in the mistaken belief that these views, terms and desires constitute our identity; our "shoulds," then, are an assertion of who we think we are.

Think, for example, of the woman, shouting at her mother, "You never would let me have a black dress, and I always wanted one." For fifteen or twenty years, this woman has cherished the thought that her mother should have bought her a black dress. She identifies herself, then, partly as "that-girl-who-was-deprived-of-the-dress-she-should-have-had." The self-confirmatory nature of those thoughts is demonstrated by the intensity with which she has clung to this minor issue over the years. But it can only pack the self-confirmatory punch as long as it is supported by the "should." The moment she becomes aware that there is no "should" at all, that it is existentially totally irrelevant whether she ever got or ever gets a black dress, the whole drama trails away like a punctured balloon. And that could be uncomfortable, embarrassing. To discover that one has been making an enormous to-do over nothing for twenty years is embarrassing. Some folk will hang onto their to-dos for their entire lives, rather than face the embarrassment of realizing their nothingness.

So, we cling to our "shoulds" and "should-nots," not because they are constructive guides, but because they keep our sense of being particular and important persons going. When others, moving around in their own, private world of private "shoulds," fail to fit in with our "shoulds," we become upset and blame the people involved. We can observe should-thinking at the root of many marital problems.

Ryan came storming into his session full of what he considered to be "righteous" indignation, not to mention rage. He thought he had a plum for the counselor, one which would clearly demonstrate what awful things he had to put up with in living with his wife. Just before he had left for work that morning, he had gone into the bathroom and there discovered that his wife's dog had "left something on the bathroom floor." "So I told her," he said. "I said, 'Your dog left something on the bathroom floor. Make sure you clean it up.' And you know what? You know what? When I came home tonight at six o'clock, the mess was still there. Can you believe it? Can you imagine? She left it there the whole day, after I told her to clean it up."

The counselor responded quietly, "Why didn't you clean it up when you discovered it?" "Me?" he bellowed. "Me? Why should I clean it up? It's her dog. And it's her job to keep the house clean. So why should I clean it up? *She* should clean it up."

He thinks he is very upset by his wife's behavior. But he is really upset by his own should-thoughts. If the should-thoughts disappeared, his rage would disappear, and he would be free to respond intelligently and helpfully to whatever situations arise in his home as well as elsewhere.

Marriage is the prime arena of should-thinking. It almost seems as if we think that there is a clause in the marriage ceremony which declares: "I now pronounce you man and wife and bestow upon you ever hereafter, until death do you part, the right to 'should' one another unmercifully." As we have explored in the last chapter, the basic, most troublesome "should" of marriage is the belief: My husband or wife should meet my needs. Not only cannot another individual meet our needs, but often what are considered to be needs are nothing more than "shoulds." So the real belief is: My husband or wife should gratify all my shoulds. Here we have a super-should which is guaranteed to make for endless trouble.

Two young wives were recently discussing their frustration and impatience over their husbands' failures to share household tasks and responsibilities. "We don't expect them to do anything unreasonable," they protested. "We just think they should share doing things around the house. Of course, *they* think *we* should do everything at home because they work," the wives exclaimed in obvious disbelief at the naiveté of the men's expectations. "But who are they to tell us what we should do with our time? We share home life together and therefore they should share the tasks that are involved." Totally exasperated by their husbands' "shoulds," these young women remained blind to their own. When confronted with the idea of trying to evaluate the issue on the basis of what is needed, intelligent and loving, they remained stuck in the should-context: "But why should we have to do everything while they sit around and loaf? Why should we be the ones to give in?"

"Shoulds" lead to interpersonal (intershouldal?) power

struggles, and in the battle of the "shoulds," unintelligence reigns. The young wives are saying to their husbands, "Things are not right around here and you are to blame"— to which, of course, the young husbands reply, "You bet things are not right, but it is you who are to blame." In the "you should, no, *you* should" game, harmonious resolution is made impossible by the fact that the game requires a winner-loser outcome. Somebody must "give in" to the other, a degrading act, and one which, understandably, both sides resist as long as possible.

Interpersonal "shoulding" may be easier to spot and recognize as invalid than what might be termed "existential shoulding." It seems entirely natural for us to assume that we know what our lives should be and to cherish thoughts about what we should become. Who would even question a thought like "I should be happy"? And that happiness takes on specific definitions by individuals: "I should be successful . . . married . . . a parent . . . not married . . . not a parent . . . busy . . . not busy," etc., ad infinitum.

We have discovered, though, that should-thinking is made up of dangerous elements: negative judgment, personal condemnations, a belief that the good is not now and that whoever or whatever should be bringing it about is failing to do so. It is to be expected, then, that the emotional counterparts of should-thinking will necessarily consist of discouragement, depression, frustration, resentment, and anger. Since should-thinking is the thought-pattern belonging to ego-consciousness, which dwells in the limited, changing, never-perfect world, what "should be" never comes into final expression. Like "tomorrow," it never comes. Things never, finally, arrive at what they "should be." Any gratification of a "should" or "should not" is temporary and soon replaced by a new dissatisfaction. When one lives oriented toward should-thinking, one's happiness is in moment-by-moment jeopardy. For a should-thinker suffers from every instance in which his experience does not coincide with his should-thought. And if it is not the weather, or other drivers on the highway, or other riders on the bus or subway, or what is served for supper, or his own height or weight, it will be something else that is not as it "should be." Should-thinking hurts. A should-thought always yields dissatisfaction, and it is not a solvable dissatisfaction, because its source is not in Reality; it is in the basic pattern of thought. Therefore, unless we come to recognize the true source of the dissatisfaction, we will be subject to endless complaints and wild-goose chases.

Not a few divorces are the consequence, at least in part, of the mistaken belief that the marriage is the cause of the feelings of dissatisfaction which one or both partners are experiencing. The popular mid-life crisis, in which men are particularly prone to leave their wives and families and/or change professions, is fraught with secret shoulds: "I am not as happy as I should be. I am not as fulfilled as I should be. My work is not as interesting . . . exciting . . . remunerative as it should be. My sex life is not as satisfying as it should be. My marriage should not be so lifeless or boring or in a rut. My husband should not just sit in front of the TV . . . or play tennis every Saturday . . . or work so much." And on and on and on.

If we recognize that the frustration and restlessness are rooted in our thoughts about what should or should not be, then we will be able to find the Source of good, and our lives can unfold wholesomely. But if we believe our "shoulds," we are in big trouble.

Some months ago, I went through a period of considerable dissatisfaction and frustration. Even though I knew better, my thoughts would gravitate toward ideas of what was wrong which were very much abroad in our culture: "My life is too determined by my husband's schedule and the family's demands. I should have more freedom, time for myself." And so on. The more I focused on these complaints and fantasized possible solutions, the more aggravated and frustrated I felt.

One day, during a period of meditation, I thought of the second principle, and the words "the good of God already is" came to mind. Suddenly my consciousness was flooded with a realization of what a wonderful husband, family, and life I have. I saw clearly the dissatisfaction as the fruit of dwelling on opinions about what "should be" and "should not be" which were entirely unrelated to my actual situation. I realized that, while I was entirely free to make any changes in my schedule which might be needed, what I really needed was to dwell, in consciousness, on the abundant good which already is. At that time, I was completely healed of the frustration and dissatisfaction. Once free from them, I was struck by the seductive power of the popular "shoulds" and "should nots." It seems likely that many divorces are not authentic resolutions of unhealthy situations but simply a consequence of blind entanglement in the currently popular judgments about "what's wrong"—the cultural should-thinking of our day.

We can be saved from making troublesome mistakes by knowing that our lives are none of our business. This is a somewhat dramatic way of stating the concept of "shouldlessness." Shouldlessness does not refer to wishy-washy, directionless or fatalistic attitudes toward life. It means recognizing that we are being lived by a Life which lives to bloom; that the process of blooming is governed by an Intelligence which governs the harmonious expression of all Being, which knows all, sees all. Even a glimpse of the magnitude and perfection of divine Being leads us to recognize the ridiculous audacity of the ego in presuming to be able to know what is best for us. A glimpse of transcendental awareness reduces us, like Job, to a humble silence. We become willing, even grateful, to seek a consciousness of good and to let that good govern our lives.

The problem, as we have noted, is that when we try to run our lives, we are actually not running them, we are giving them over to ideas from the sea of mental garbage. This bears repeating, because to the unenlightened mind nothing is so certain as that "I am me." But the "me" that I think I am is not only not the real "me," but she is not even my friend. "She" is no real individual at all, but rather a counterfeit identity, built up from mistaken perceptions. To say, then, that my life is none of my business is to recognize that the ego with its personal sense cannot adequately or authentically govern my affairs and lead them in the direction which will be life-enhancing.

The woman quoted in the chapter on Omniaction, who describes, after her enlightenment, the sense of her life being guided and governed by "a consciousness which is neither myself nor not myself" but which is "protecting or leading me into directions helpful to my proper growth and maturity, and propelling me away from that which is against that growth," came to that awareness after a clear loss of her identification with her ego. Describing the moment of her awakening, she says,

> Slowly my focus changed: "I'm dead! There's nothing to call *me*! There never was a *me*! It's an allegory, a mental image, a pattern upon which nothing was ever modeled!" I grew dizzy with delight. . . . Everything my eyes fell upon was radiantly beautiful.[2]

Some people defend their egos to the death, yet our egos tell us terrible lies about ourselves and reality, and it is

2. Philip Kapleau, ed., *The Three Pillars of Zen* (Boston: Beacon Press, 1965), p. 267.

the ego which must "die" if we would know the "radiant beauty" of Reality. Significantly, the death of this woman's ego was not the death of her sense of being an individual. Quite the contrary, it firmly established her true identity. "There is nothing to do," she writes in awe. "Just to be is a supremely total act." True identity needs no "doing" props to continually secure it; it is firmly established on the basis of Being.

Your life is none of your business. You did not create it and you have no way of knowing what it "should" be. You may, however, gratefully and humbly discover what it *is*. Your identity is like a treasure chest which it is your privilege to open and delight in. This is done by asking, "What and who am I as God knows me?" It is only what Love-Intelligence knows of us which is real.

Likewise, your marriage is none of your business. It, too, is the business of Love-Intelligence. You cannot make your marriage good by any personal efforts based on ideas of what "should" or "should not" be. The dreadful machinations recommended in some popular "womanhood" books and courses are transparently invalid. Supposed to enhance the marriage, they become admittedly attempts to bring a husband under the wife's secret control by playing on the man's assumed vanity and lust. Such calculations will backfire, for we reap what we sow.

We know what we want, but we rarely know what we really need. Moreover, our ideas about what is available and possible for us are very much circumscribed by past experiences, translated into our basic assumptions about life. Therefore, the best that we can even imagine for ourselves remains very, very limited.

Eric Butterworth tells, in one of his books, a true story of a poor woman from a village in Europe who scrimps and saves for years to get enough money to visit her son in the United States. She purchases her boat ticket and spends ten days or so sailing across the Atlantic. Her poverty-stricken consciousness and ignorance lead her to spend the entire time in her cabin, subsisting on a basket of food which she brought along with her, unable to imagine, in her wildest dreams, that a feast is available to her three times a day, in the ship's dining room, paid for in her ticket. Thus are we blind to the good that can be ours. Auntie Mame says it a bit more pithily: "Life is a banquet and most poor (suckers) are starving to death."

Love and "should" cannot co-exist; they are mutually exclusive. Love looks to see the good; "should" looks to see the bad and to blame somebody. Moreover, when our "should" is directed toward others, we violate their basic integrity. We are trying to make them characters in our little personal dramas of life; we are trying to usurp the role of God in their lives. Our husbands, wives, children and parents are not in the world to please us, to give us what we want, to be what we think they "should" be. They are God's beloved children, and their destinies are between them and God. It is blasphemous for us to think we have the right to interfere.

The danger of self-righteous "shoulding" is probably greatest for spiritual seekers. The sneaky "shoulds" of the spiritual quest are often difficult to spot in one's own thinking. The most obvious is the assumption that the rest of the family "should" be on the same path that I am. How can we possibly know that? The spiritual affairs of another are holy and private territory. We may, if asked, share the goodness which we have found in a particular path. But we may never, validly, purport to tell another that he or she should think what we think, do what we do. (This does not mean that we are to give our children no specific guidance in spiritual matters. That issue will be discussed in Chapter 8.)

If our path is a valid one, then we will be finding and demonstrating in our lives increasing serenity, joy, love and abundance. If we truly leave our family members free, they may be attracted by the values and qualities which show through us and may seek them, either in the particular form of our search or in another form, more authentic to their needs. But if we have in any way regarded ourselves as "the right" or "the good" or "the spiritual" one in the family, we have established an enormous barrier to the spiritual quest for other family members.

In metapsychiatry, it is understood that an enlightened individual becomes "a beneficial presence in the world." This is very different from being a beneficent person. The presence of a beneficent person conveys the message, "See how very good and wonderful I am." The presence of a beneficial presence conveys the message, "See how very good and wonderful Life is." One of the best illustrations of a beneficial presence comes out of the Zen tradition. After enlightenment, the enlightened one remains a humble figure, indistinguishable from others, except for the fact that wherever he walks, "the dead trees come to life."

If we are seekers, what we seek to see is the good of God everywhere. When we look at our spouses, children, and parents, we seek to see through the masks of their personhood to the loveliness of their true being. That is love. And that is what causes us to bloom, as well as our loved ones and, finally, even the dead trees.

In her extraordinary book, *Whole Child, Whole Parent,* Polly Berends writes:

> True love begins with the simple desire to be good. It proceeds with the conscious affirmation and discovery of goodness. It ends or is fulfilled in the realization that there is nothing but goodness

and that there never was anything else in the first place. Love is the accurate perception of the truth of being.

Applying this to the nitty-gritty of life with an infant, she writes:

> The baby is dirty all the time. We are constantly changing his diapers and wiping his bottom. And yet it is so easy to see that he is pure. All that defecating has nothing to do with him; he doesn't even know about it. And all that ignorance of the mess he is making doesn't have anything to do with him either; he will learn. We are not at all deceived by the mess into thinking that he is either impure or stupid. We have never seen such purity! No matter what he does to sheets, diapers, clothes or our laps, purity remains to us an obvious characteristic of the child's true self.
>
> The purity we see—that's truth. And the distinguishing we do between the purity and the mess, that's love. . . . Love is the sorting out in thought of the perfect child from all suggestions to the contrary.[3]

When it is our husband or wife, rather than an infant, it may seem to be more difficult to see through the "mess" to the spiritual qualities. The more we take the negative aspects of their behavior personally, the more difficult it is for us to even want to see through to their true being. That's when the "shoulds" and "should nots" tempt us

---

3. Polly Berrien Berends, *Whole Child, Whole Parent* (New York: Harper's Magazine Press, 1975), pp. 224, 226-27.

most. How can we not think that our spouse should not do something which bothers us and may even seem to do us damage? It is only understanding that can free us. When we understand the degree to which it is our should-thinking that is the source of our discomfort, rather than the behavior of the other, we become very interested in seeking first the already-good and being liberated from the "shoulds."

Alice's story is a dramatic illustration of this. A young mother with two small children, she came for help with chronic depression. She was, indeed, depressed—crushingly, continually depressed. She was underweight, being often unable to eat; withdrawn, never leaving the house except for necessary shopping; always fatigued and on the edge of desperation. In the first interview, she told of her husband Arnold who, when the two children were to be born, just dropped her off at the door of the hospital and went home to watch TV. She felt absolutely crushed by his behavior and blamed him and his "lovelessness" for her depression. All she could think about was, "He shouldn't do that to me. He shouldn't just dump me when I need him. He should take care of me, sit with me, be with me. That's what he would do if he loved me."

Alice failed to keep her next appointment. She had had a sudden serious illness and had been rushed to the hospital. Some months later, she returned. I scarcely recognized her. She had gained weight, was vivacious and happy. She reported that she was now active in church and school and everything was going well. What had happened?

The evening of her illness, Arnold had again gone through his dumping routine, delivering her to the emergency room and then leaving. But this time, something different happened in Alice's consciousness. The thought popped into her mind, "Well, that's Arnold for you!" Not, "He should have stayed," but "That's Arnold for you." In that moment, she was liberated from the belief that her husband's behavior deprived her of love, for his boorish behavior was a deprivation to her only as long as she held onto the thought that he should do something else. She felt, in spite of the seriousness of her physical condition, a tremendous euphoria. She thought she overheard a doctor and a nurse paying her a compliment. She felt surrounded by love and goodness, felt herself to be valued and appreciated. She was soon well, and the healing of her depression remained as well as the healing of her body. She spontaneously realized "the good of God which already is" the moment the should-thinking about Arnold, which had blocked it out of her consciousness, ceased.

The thought that somebody should be different or do things differently is an altogether troublesome thought. Nobody is benefited by it. This is equally true when the somebody is oneself. In the spiritual quest, self-shoulding is a major monkey-wrench. Whether the supposed goal is enlightenment or salvation or PAGL (peace, assurance, gratitude, love—the signs in consciousness, according to metapsychiatry, of at-onement with spiritual consciousness), goal-oriented thinking too easily turns into the depressing thought that one is not yet where one should be spiritually, or has not yet achieved what should have been achieved. Spiritual ambition, which is based upon the belief that spiritual growth is a personal achievement, is an exceedingly dangerous thing, for it is so easily disguised as a laudatory spiritual zeal.

How can we tell whether we are being single-minded or are motivated by "shoulds"? There is a simple test which will invariably tell us whether or not our thoughts are valid. We ask: "Is my thinking God-confirmatory or self-confirmatory?" Self-confirmatory thinking is easy to spot by the presence of "I": "How am I doing? How am I? Am I where I should be?" etc. Spiritual ambition is a personal drive to achieve a good which is not yet achieved. Single-mindedness is a single-minded concern to see the good which already is.

The second principle is a very helpful and useful one in exposing the secret "shoulds" of the spiritual quest. Whenever a thought comes into my mind which reflects a "should" relating to spiritual concerns, such as, "I should be able to see that by now," "I shouldn't still be interested in that," or even, "I shouldn't be thinking should-thoughts," I counter it with, "But the good of God already is. Therefore everything is already all right." This leads me to be able to see that even the spiritual quest can become a drama for the ego to feed on, and any personal drama, even a spiritual personal drama, is unreal. The already-isness of the good of God cuts through should-thinking on any level.

By seeing what already is, we become it; by seeing what already is, we help others become it. Nothing so potentiates the actualization of good in our human experience as a focus in consciousness upon seeing the perfect spiritual Reality which lies behind all the appearances. The most loving thing we can do for our husbands or wives is to pray for them the "prayer of beholding."[4] Quakers have described intercessory prayer as "holding someone in the Light." The prayer of beholding is something like that. It consists in mentally beholding the individual in the context of God. In our minds we separate the individual in his true being from the ignorant thoughts which he or she has unwittingly picked up. Seeing these thoughts as just thoughts and as not related in any essential way to the individual—they are not his or her thoughts, but sea-of-mental-garbage thoughts—tends to free us to behold the

---

4. Thomas Hora, *Existential Metapsychiatry* (New York: The Seabury Press, 1977), Session No. 4, p. 18. See also the *Dialogues*, Chapters 2, 11 and 12.

spiritual being which makes up that individual's true identity. Keeping that image of perfect spiritual identity in our minds is a very potent practice and is the most helpful thing we can do for another.

Where "should" is, good is not. Where good is, "should" is not. Moment-by-moment it is our choice: Will our marriages be our business, arenas of "shoulds" with their endless conflicts, endless dissatisfactions? Or will our marriages be God's business, arenas where the love and intelligence, peace and joy, harmony and vitality of existential Reality take shape and form in human experience?

SUMMARY

"Take no thought for what should be or what should not be; seek ye first to know the good of God, which already is" (Principle 2 of Metapsychiatry).

• The good which we need for the health and harmony of married life is not something we can manufacture; it can only be discovered.

• This good is "God's good," meaning that it is spiritual Reality, existing now and discovered when we realize a spiritual level of consciousness.

• Ideas about what should or should not be are negative, blaming, and wedded to a view of reality which perpetuates dissatisfaction and difficulty.

• If we believe that our marriages are our business, to be conducted along the lines of what we think should and should not be, we have abandoned them to the-sea-of mental-garbage, and they will relentlessly demonstrate their mental source.

• When we concern ourselves with seeing the good which already is, rather than trying to remedy what we think is bad, then that good takes over the running of our marriages and they become showcases for the good which we see.

6. Sex and Love in Marriage

"If you know what, you know how" (Principle 6 of Metapsychiatry).

"Yes is good, but no is also good" (Principle 4 of Metapsychiatry).

As originally conceived, this book would not have had a separate chapter on sex. That may seem strange in a book about marriage, but it is appropriate. In a marriage which is based upon a mutual concern with realizing and participating in the good of God, sex is no big deal, and neither is it a problem. It is simply one aspect of a harmonious life together. I had expected to discuss sexual issues as they arose in conjunction with the discussion of the basic issues and principles of married life.

But that clearly will not do. Having just finished watching a series on the TV news dealing with sex therapy, I am reminded once again that there is a colossal process of sexual miseducation taking place which needs to be addressed. The glorification of sensualism goes unchecked and unquestioned in our society today, and it is not only unquestioned, but wholeheartedly supported by the physicians, psychologists, counselors and ministers who are the oracles of our culture. We look to the "doctors"—M.D., Ph.D., D.D.—to guide us on matters basic to our life and well-being. But that may be a risky thing to do. A culture's "experts" usually end up being spokesmen or spokeswomen of the cultural fads of the day, and that is certainly true with regard to sex at this time. A fraud is being perpetrated on the public, with the enthusiastic support of the media, and married life is where the negative fallout from the deceit is most destructively felt.

The problem with the mistaken views on sex is compounded by the culture-wide failure to understand what love is. The meaning of the word "love" is distorted on all sides: by sensualism, by interpersonalism, and also by misguided religious believers. Rather than being a reliable guide in sexual and personal matters, then, love becomes a term used to rationalize and support all kinds of ideas and behavior which have nothing to do with love at all.

The principle, "If you know what, you know how," though originally formulated as a guide to the spiritual quest, is remarkably pertinent to sex as well. Taken physiologically, the principle becomes a rather humorous dismissal of the endless "how-to" sex manuals, which tend to turn the bedroom into a circus tent. But more importantly, it leads our thinking into fruitful channels for making sense out of all the ideas which bombard us. What is sex? What is its nature and its function in human life? What is love? And what is its nature and function in human life? When we get those "what's" answered, we'll find most of our other questions answered as well.

Let's look at love, first, for it is of preeminent value. (See, also, the discussions of love in Chapters 4 and 5.) Love is a primary divine attribute. In metapsychiatry, the favored term for God is "Love-Intelligence," indicating that Love is a central aspect of the Fundamental Order of Reality. To say it more simply, Love is a law of Life. Love and

Life are inseparable; you can't have one without the other. Brought down into everyday experience, this means, first of all, that we are never deprived of love, no matter what the appearance of things. And it means that a consciousness of love is at the heart of wholesome living. Love is of primary importance as both a motive and a value: it is something we must be and something we must see in order to live. The desire to be loving coupled with the desire to see Love puts us in harmony with Life and leads us to live in such a way that things go well for us.

A loving individual is one who looks for the good in other people and in life and, by seeing goodness, becomes a channel for it. A loving individual wants the best, for himself or herself and for others. This does not mean that he or she wants to please or gratify himself or herself or others but that he or she wants to participate in the spiritual qualities which bloom lives.

Love always goes with intelligence; there is no such thing as "stupid" love, and that helps us clarify what is loving and what is not. A woman who thinks that it is "love" which keeps her chained to an affair with a married man can be sure that it is not love, but lust or insecurity or an ignorance of the good which is available to her that is really at work. A man who says that he is too loving and that consequently other people walk all over him is not talking about love but about an attempt to get other people to like him by inviting them to exploit him. Parents who never say "no" to a child because they want to "let love rule" are not loving; they are simply ignorant of the child's need for structure. Love is always intelligent and therefore it is always genuinely good for everybody involved. If it ever seems that "love" leads you into self-defeating situations or makes life problematic for others, then be sure that it is not love but something else which is operating in consciousness.

Love, then, is not the same thing as what is termed

"romantic love." That is not love; it is personal attraction, personal admiration, feeling-good-together, sometimes mutual appetite. It is, as we all know, very unreliable and fleeting. It is based on the momentary illusion that another person meets our deepest need. Because it is an illusion, it is sure to let us down. Not only pride "goeth before a fall" but also romantic "love." Romance and sex are virtually synonymous. (Just watch "The Love Boat" on TV.) But love has no essential connection to sex at all.

Real love is not an emotion, and it has no object; it is a state of consciousness in which the spiritual truth of being is cherished, and others and all of life are seen in that light. It makes one supremely intelligent and capable of discerning real needs, and of responding appropriately to them. Love is spiritual, and its nature and function are the blooming of all life.

There are several terms relating to sex which need to be distinguished. When we talk about "sex" we are usually talking about genital sexual activity. When we talk about "sexuality" we are usually talking about an individual's gender-identity: maleness, femaleness, masculinity, femininity. Recently, the terms "sensual" and "sensuality" have come into frequent usage. They are used in a way which implies that they are valuable qualities to be cultivated and sought after. "Sensual" actually means "of the body and the senses as distinguished from the intellect or spirit" and "sensuality" means "a fondness for or indulgence in sensual pleasures."

Existentially speaking, sex is no problem and sexuality is no problem, but sensualism—that's a problem. It is a problem of consciousness, and it is because of our understanding of the importance of consciousness in our lives that we can see what a problem sensualism is. Sensualism is a focus, in consciousness, upon bodies and bodily sensations. It is a problem because it keeps one's attention riveted to the grossest level of experience and identity, a level which is fraught with difficulty and suffering. And, of course, it thus blinds one to the spiritual values and qualities which are so necessary to human fulfillment.

What we see in our culture today is the backlash to Victorian sexual repression, a backlash which, as is always the case, goes to the opposite extreme without ever examining the real underlying issue. The underlying belief is the same today as it was in Victorian times. It is the belief that sex is Important. For, whether one must suppress and repress all sexual feelings and interests because they are so Bad, or whether one must express one's sexual feelings and preoccupations because they are so Good, the assumption remains that sex is Important.

In our day, it is precisely "sex" that is considered to be a big deal, not sexuality in any larger sense. There is the belief that engaging in sexual activities with others is very important and "healthy," that it is such activity which fulfills one as a man or woman. Being able to "achieve orgasm" and being able to "turn your partner on" are values promoted at large. The cultural valuing of sex is particularly revealed by the rapid rise of "sex therapy" which amounts to the "scientific" blessing of the culture's backlash. Once we have a physician and a psychologist, in white coats, teaching people, in a clinic, with straight faces, how to learn to be sensual, any hope of maintaining some perspective in the matter is down the drain.

What is lacking in the cultural picture is an understanding of life which offers a larger context within which to view sex. Sexual behavior and activity, like all human behavior and activity, are manifestations of a mentality: the physical expresses the mental. Sex, then, is not a physiological "need" like eating and drinking, and the so-called sex "drive" is not physiologically determined. Sexual appetite has everything to do with the level of consciousness of the individual. Sex, like every other aspect of material and personal existence, has no goodness or value in and of itself. It becomes a channel for expressing the basic values of those involved. It is valuable, then, only to the extent that it is used as a channel for the good of God, which means it is good only so long as love and intelligence, kindness and patience, joy and beauty are involved.

When sexual activities and practices are governed by sensualism, they become problematic. Sensualism gives one no healthy or intelligent standard for sexual behavior. Whatever "turns one on" is "good"; if something is physically gratifying, "the more, the better." A sensualist tends to view others as bodies, also, and when other bodies cease to gratify him or her, the sensualist has no further interest in them. When sensualism governs a relationship, inside or outside marriage, the growth of that relationship is inevitably stunted. There is simply not room in consciousness for the nurturing of delicate, aesthetic values, for a growth of awareness of good and lovely things. Sensualism is a mental narcotic, and sensual sex poisons a marriage; it does not enhance it.

In the Roman Catholic Church, the marriage union, including the sexual union, is declared to be sacramental: a "means of grace" or a channel of God's blessing into human affairs. The teaching remains a valuable pointer to the preeminence of spiritual values in wholesome living. It does not mean that if you have a certain ritual done in the right church, your sexual intercourse will therefore make you holy or will automatically be blessed and harmonious. It does mean that marriage, with all its intimacies, needs to be lived in the context of God in order for it to be life-enhancing and health-producing, in order for it to receive and participate in the beauty, vitality and health which are appropriate. And it also means that when the union of a man and a woman is hallowed—committed to the good of

God—then it becomes a means of grace for the potentiation of good blesses all those involved.

A "good sex life" has nothing to do with frequency of intercourse or orgasms. Just keeping the activity going is no big deal. But to keep the loving, the affection and thoughtfulness and humor and playfulness in sex over the years—now that's something. Egos just can't do that on their own. God is absolutely essential to keeping a good sex life good. There is an unimaginable discipline involved in living with someone, sleeping in the same bedroom with him or her every night for years and keeping that bedroom atmosphere harmonious and healthy. People who opt for a celibate life style may tend to regard married folk as less spiritual or less disciplined than they, but that view is at least questionable. For anyone interested in it, marriage offers as consistent a spiritual discipline as any purposely devised. The ego—the complaining, demanding, protesting, self-seeking, counterfeit sense of self—must yield to God, to the spiritual facts of being, for the marriage, and the sex within it, to be wholly good. Like all other "ego-goods," "good sex" turns bad unless the good which it manifests is "the good of God."

A good sex life, then, can involve a good deal of sexual intercourse or none at all. It will not necessarily satisfy the sensual desires of the partners, because the partners will not be concerned, first of all, with getting their "itches scratched." A good sex life means that the whole physical dimension of life together will be characterized by gentleness, affection, consideration and generosity, with a marked absence of friction and self-seeking.

As a footnote, we might add that in a home where the physical dimension of life together is governed by spiritual values, the children are being provided with the best sex education possible. It is far more important for children to learn to associate the physical with these loving and benevolent qualities than it is for them to learn the precise physiological details of sexual intercourse. Sex apart from the good of God can become an awful thing. When we are more interested in the good of God than in sex, then sex is sanctified by the spiritual good in which it participates.

In an existentially valid marriage, the nature and function of sex are subservient to the nature and function of the marriage. In other words, in a marriage which is a joint quest for spiritual growth and a joint participation in the good of God, sexual activity will be engaged in for the sake of the larger goals. Some austere religious life styles permit sexual intercourse only for the procreation of children. In our view, sex is valid as an expression of love and for the purpose of freeing consciousness from physical preoccupation.

Practically speaking, most marriages tend to get into ruts which are largely determined by the demands of work, children and housekeeping. Ways of treating each other also tend to become somewhat patterned as the years go on. In a busy household, expressions of affection and appreciation—the light and gentle touches which are so enhancing to a life partnership—can be forgotten, even though the thoughts are there. Times of sexual togetherness provide an opportunity for the expression of gratitude and affection between partners, what I call the "smoochy-goochies," and when sexual intercourse is cherished and kept for that purpose, it enhances a marriage.

Many sex therapists would say that the enhancement of loving communication between husband and wife is precisely their goal in the teaching of sensual techniques. That may well be. But sensualism is a tricky business. It is far better to focus on spiritual qualities such as love and gratitude and generosity in learning to communicate lovingly in sex than to focus on pleasure. It is my experience that a desire to be loving and generous and appreciative does more for the enhancement of sex than any sensual technique could possibly do.

A spiritual focus does not repudiate sex; it sanctifies it. Not only is the quality of sexual activity improved, but, even more important, sex then tends to contribute to the overall quest for spiritual growth rather than detract from it. Since consciousness is the issue, we can see that the sexual issue is not "doing it or not doing it," but rather "thinking about it or not thinking about it." An individual may be celibate, yet preoccupied with sexual fantasies all day long. In that case, his celibacy profits him nothing, for his consciousness remains chained to the flesh. The same is true of the married man or woman who thinks about sex all the time. The spiritual seeker desires to become increasingly free from thoughts which focus on himself or herself as a body. Consequently, sexual activity is not pursued for its own sake, for the indulgence of the body, but for the releasing of consciousness. When intercourse partakes of spiritual qualities, as described above, then the physiological release involved is also a release in consciousness of physical preoccupation. Frequency of practice is determined by the partner's discovery of what provides for optimal freedom of consciousness for the recognizing of spiritual realities.

The principle "Yes is good and no is also good" demonstrates an enlightened state of mind which is reverently responsive to what arises, moment by moment, neither grabbing nor pushing away the events or people which unfold in one's daily experience. Like Principle 6, it can usefully be applied to a discussion of sex. For the essence of this state of consciousness is an absence of ego-concern, of willfulness. And such an absence is "devoutly to be wished" in sexual matters.

Apart from spiritual concern, sex can only be self-centered. If I see sex to be for the purpose of bodily relief or gratification, then my motive becomes willful: to get what I want when I want it from somebody else. Then "yes" and "no" become important, and married couples often polarize into the "yes-sayer" and the "no-sayer." The "yes-sayer" wants sex to gratify his or her desires; the "no-sayer" doesn't "feel like it," meaning that sex wouldn't gratify his or her desires which take a different form and require gratification of another sort.

Sex, as we have said, is not per se a problem, but the ego always is. And so when ego concerns govern the sexual realm in marriage, sex becomes troublesome. If we find that "yes" and "no" are important to us in relation to sex, we will know that ego has crept in, and we can re-evaluate our concerns at that moment. If we go with the ego trip by way of sex at that moment, insisting upon our "yes" or "no" out of willfulness, we will have to live with some negative fallout afterward, both in our own consciousness and perhaps from our partner. Ego triggers ego, and, furthermore, if you give ego an inch, it takes a mile. Put those two aphorisms together and you have the ego-equivalent of a nuclear chain reaction.

"Yes is good and no is also good." Sex is not, per se, important. So if it unfolds, lovingly and harmoniously, that is good, and if it does not, that is also good. There is no need to insist, either way. Keeping this principle in mind when issues relating to sex arise in marriage is a very practical and helpful tool for saving our sex lives from the poisonous pollution of ego.

This principle does not mean, however, that one must go along with whatever one's partner desires. A commitment to these principles of intelligent living never requires us to give in to unhealthy behavior in other people, because that is not intelligent. Such a commitment, in fact, sometimes requires us to take a stand, based upon principle, which may displease our spouses. But if the stand is genuinely a matter of spiritual commitment, then it will bless us and our loved ones as well. A "yes" or "no" based upon a discernment of what is valid and needed at the moment is a very different matter from a "yes" or "no" based on will-fulness. For ourselves, it is the willfulness we need to look out for.

The principle means that the issue to be considered is not whether or not you "feel like" having sex at the moment. The valid existential issue in sex, as in everything else, is whether you are prepared to respond, with both intelligence and consideration, to your partner's concern.

When spiritual values come first, sex falls into place. Sex problems, therefore, are not really sex problems. They are, like all human problems, indications that we are somehow out of whack with Life, and the solution needs to be sought in our thinking and knowing. Instead of sex therapy, we need love therapy, for "love is the accurate perception of the truth of being." In that accurate perception lies the healing of all our problems and the fulfilling of our true potential as well. Perhaps someday we will learn that no matter what aspect of human life we are concerned with, God can "fix" it and God can "run" it a lot better than we can.

7. Problem-Solving in Marriage

"God helps those who let him" (Principle 5 of Meta-psychiatry).

"Problems are lessons designed for our edification" (Principle 8 of Metapsychiatry).

In a sense, a separate chapter on problem-solving might seem to be unnecessary, even inappropriate. Everything discussed so far has to do with problem-solving. To be concerned with the spiritualization of consciousness, to be focused on seeking to know Reality, is unequivocably the most efficient way both to resolve and to prevent problems. Problem-free living is a by-product of spiritual seeing. The focus is on the seeing; spiritual seeing solves.

Most of us, though, still consciously struggle with problems in our lives and in our marriages. And metapsychiatry, perhaps because it is the fruit of a psychiatric practice, speaks directly to the issue of problem-solving and offers a great deal of specific guidance in how to intelligently understand and respond to the appearance of problems in our lives.

The problems of marriage take on a special form and

focus which reflect the special situation of marriage. Likewise, the marital situation stimulates certain special mistakes in attempting to solve problems. Perhaps obviously, these mistakes have to do with the seemingly unending *two*ness of marriage, the unique situation of perpetual partnership in daily life. Only with a husband or wife is there this sense of "foreverness" in our living together. Our children grow up and leave; our parents grow old and pass on; our friends come and go over the years; but if we take marriage seriously, our spouse is "forever" (which is how long it seems "till death us do part").

What kind of problems, then, and what kind of mistakes in problem-solving are specific, though not exclusive, to marriage? Metapsychiatry offers a list of "six futile questions" which we tend to ask when a problem arises. These are: (1) What's wrong? (2) How do I feel? (3) Why? (4) Who's to blame? (5) What do I do about it? (6) How do I do it?[1] In marriage, the emphasis tends to be on (1) What's wrong? (4) Who's to blame? and (5) What do I do about it? These questions show up in various ways in three basic marital mistakes: negativism, externalism and personalism. These mistakes are all "seeing" mistakes, a consequence of the "double-vision" (me-and-you) which plagues marriage partners.

The first mistake—negativism—refers to the fact that inevitably, in marriage, there is a tendency, as time goes on, to allow one's attention to be captured by a concern with what's wrong. It is essentially that which distinguishes long-term married life from the courtship and honeymoon periods. People often say that their spouses have changed radically since the beginnings of the relationship. But what has really happened is that both partners have gradually

---

1. The six futile questions and the two intelligent questions are discussed in Chapter 2 of *Dialogues in Metapsychiatry* by Thomas Hora and elsewhere throughout the book.

shifted their attention from a focus on what's right to a focus on what's wrong. That is the nature of interpersonal seeing.

In the beginning, the process of "falling in love" involves the discovery of mutuality between people which leads both individuals to feel wonderful about themselves and thus to think that the other is wonderful. It is a mutual admiration society. Probably all of us have been through that process, perhaps several times. The experience is acute: the sudden, miraculous, wonderful sense of mutual regard. It seems to heal all of our sense of inadequacy and insecurity, and we can't lavish enough adoration upon the apparent source of our bliss. Never mind that he or she is also observably this or that negative thing; that miraculous personage makes us feel glorious—so he or she is glorious.

And then comes marriage. The beginnings of twenty-four-hour living together involve something of a letdown, to be sure. Ordinary workaday life is resumed. Husband, or husband and wife, go to work and there is no longer such an intense focus upon each other. The glow usually carries over for a while; the mutual focus on what's right with each other survives the first disappointments. But the requirements of daily living make their demands felt. It didn't seem to matter, before marriage, that Mary Jo wasn't much of a cook or homemaker, but now that Barney has to get his own breakfast every morning and comes home after work to a messy house and a dinner of canned spaghetti, it matters. It didn't seem so important, before marriage, that Ralph always wanted to know where Becky was; in fact, it made her feel really desirable and loved. But now that Becky can't even have lunch with a male co-worker without a big explosion on Ralph's part, it matters. Something is *wrong*.

And so the shift in perspective takes place, and each partner, increasingly aware that his or her whole life from now on is at stake, begins to register more and more distinctly the negative aspects of the other's behavior. And in that perspective, your spouse is no longer seen as the source of good feelings about yourself, but rather as a source of bad feelings, as a threat to the good. Your whole life has changed, and not for the good, as you thought, but for the bad. You have been betrayed. And there you are—stuck.

The first marital mistake—the focus on what's wrong— is actually the inevitable consequence of the romantic focus upon what's right, that is, of seeing the other as a source of total and perpetual satisfaction. If "you light up my life," then you can also, presumably, darken it. As we discussed in Chapter 3, false personal expectations of another lead to disillusionment—and also to the other two marital mistakes.

Externalism and personalism go together. Interpersonal negativism leads us to locate our problems outside ourselves, in our partners. It is virtually impossible for married people not to think, when things seem not to be going well between them, that the problem would be solved if only the spouse would change in some way. It is so easy to see what is wrong with one's husband or wife that it seems obvious that if he or she would correct that fault, things would be better. Although often accompanied by disclaimers such as "Oh, I know I'm not perfect either," the attitude of both partners who come for marriage counseling is almost always that it is the other who must change. There is a secret hope, lurking in the mind of each, that the counselor will be able, finally, to shape the other up.

The externalization of the problem, then, leads us to assume that the way to solve the problem is to make the partner change. This gives rise to all sorts of desperate maneuverings, calculations and manipulations in the attempt to bring about the desired change. People go to extreme lengths to try to get what they want from their spouses. In a letter to Dear Abby, one woman wrote (more tellingly than she realized), something like this: "It took a nervous breakdown to finally, after twenty years, get my husband to give me the attention and love I needed."

Part and parcel of the externalism is personalism, where my problem is seen as not only outside of me but in another person, my spouse. I take his or her behavior personally, as something he or she is doing to me, and I blame him or her personally for "hurting" me. I have a problem and he or she is personally to blame; it is his or her fault. Personalism is the Pandora's box of marriage. When you lift that lid, out spew hurt, rage, blame, guilt, murder, suicide, and every vileness one can dream of.

All three marital mistakes are illustrated in the following incident.

Barbara was extremely upset with her husband Bill. They had had a terrible fight the night before, and she was still in a state of great mental turmoil. Bill had come home from work and casually informed Barbara that he would be going to another city for a week to help open the company's new office there. He was very pleased to have been chosen for the assignment, as it represented a recognition of his capabilities and was quite an honor. He expected that Barbara, too, would be delighted. But Barbara was not delighted. She was absolutely furious. "You accepted this assignment without even asking me?" she fumed. "Just like that, you inform me that you're going to be gone for a week. You have no consideration of me at all. You don't even care what I need or what I think. All you care about is your job. Well, go on, go away for a week. I may not even be here when you get back." Not surprisingly, Bill had been stunned and had retaliated with some screaming and hollering of his own, throwing a few things for good measure, and then walking out.

Barbara's instant reaction to Bill's announcement had

been negative (she saw only what was wrong about it), external (the problem came from outside; she had been fine until Bill walked in the door and "dropped a bomb on her"), and personal (her supposedly loving husband had done something very bad to her which hurt her very much and she hated him for it and she'd get back at him if it was the last thing she did).

Much current marriage counseling is unable to be of significant help in marital problem-solving because, like the partners, it falls for the marital mistakes. It doesn't heal the negativism, personalism and externalism which cause so much difficulty; rather, it unwittingly reinforces them.

There is an overriding concern in popular marriage counseling with communication between husband and wife. The belief is that if people can learn better to "get in touch with their feelings" and to more clearly communicate these feelings to each other, a marriage will be improved. What this really does is to encourage people to dwell on their sense of what is wrong and to verbalize their complaints. One young marriage counselor told of abandoning the practice of encouraging couples to "communicate their feelings" to each other in his office because the fights got so violent that he feared for his safety—to say nothing of what happened between those couples when they got home. I was also told of a couples' group in a local church, comprised of professional people with fairly long-term marriages. The group stressed "no-holds-barred" communication, encouraging spouses to tell each other things they had never before talked about. By the end of the group, half the couples were divorced or in the process.

From an existential point of view, it is *what* we communicate that is important. The message is the medium, not vice versa. Communication which stays on the level of negativism, externalism and personalism is dynamite. Communication "techniques," whether they take the form of bonking one another with foam-rubber bats, learning to "fight fair" or simply "talking it out," will do little to facilitate health in a marriage as long as they themselves embody the very mistakes which underlie the problems.

The only communication of any value whatsoever is the communication of the truth of being. We are either "shedding light" or "shedding darkness," and when two people are jointly shedding darkness, "how great is the darkness."

Perhaps it should be said that the recognition of the inadequacy of popular marriage counseling theory to speak to real issues and heal marriages is not a personal condemnation of all counselors. In spite of the theoretical inadequacies, there are many counselors who are able to be quite helpful to people. Their helpfulness springs from their own maturity. Life is a school, and people who have lived and learned to the point of substantial maturity and wholesomeness in their own lives have learned the existential lessons and can share them helpfully with others, no matter what terms they may employ.

The three marital mistakes need correction, and they can be corrected by a commitment to what are termed the "two intelligent questions." These are: "What is the meaning of what seems to be?" and "What is what really is?" For our purposes in discussing marital issues, we'll rephrase them a bit. When confronted with a seeming marital problem, help is available when you ask:

1. What is *my* mental issue here—the lesson I need to learn?
2. What is the Reality of the situation? (What is God seeing?)

Let's take Barbara through the process of asking these questions about her "problem" and see what happens. The first question directed her attention away from Bill's behavior to her own thoughts and concerns. She began to calm down and to reflect upon what thoughts had given rise to her extreme emotional reaction. She was surprised to find herself thinking about her father, who is a traveling salesman and who was very often away from home while she was growing up, an absence which she felt as a great personal deprivation. The thought "Now Bill is going to start being away all the time" was in her mind. In addition, she discovered that she believed herself to be totally dependent upon Bill for adult companionship. The thought, "I have nobody else to talk to; I'll be all alone," was also present.

She discovered, then, that she was not really upset by Bill's brief absence on an assignment which meant an advancement at work: that was to her benefit as well as his. Her upset was the expression of the belief that she was suddenly being drastically, and probably permanently, deprived of love, support and companionship, a belief based upon her childhood ego drama and a present misguided dependency upon her husband.

She then asked the second intelligent question: What is the Reality of the situation? The second part of that question "What is God seeing?" is added in order to remind us that it is not what seems real to the ego that we seek; it is Reality as God defines it that we need to realize. When Barbara first thought about God's seeing, she pictured God looking down on her fight with Bill, and she burst out laughing. It looked so silly—the two of them screaming and throwing things and carrying on—from "up there." And then, being somewhat freed from the captivating marital movie, she began to think about her actual situation in the context of God. She was reminded of the biblical references to God as both Father and Husband, and caught a glimpse of how she had mistakenly tried to make gods (and devils) out of both her dad and Bill. The strong sense that the rug had been pulled out from under her was countered by pondering the idea of God as the Buoyancy of life and considering such statements as "underneath are the everlasting arms" and "Lord, thou has been our dwelling place in all generations." Barbara could see that her real need was not for Bill to refuse a fine assignment at work to stay home with her, but for an increased focus in her thought on the omnipresent (everywhere, all the time) availability of love, support and companionship in God. She needed to realize that her good already is, always is, in Omniactive Love-Intelligence.

By this time, Barbara had no need to ask what to do. She apologized to Bill, expressed her appreciation and gratitude that he was doing so well with his work, and shared something of what she had learned from the problem. She used her extra time during his absence to read and study spiritual literature, pray and meditate. She also made it a point to invite a girlfriend to go to a movie with her, and she had a neighbor in for a cup of tea. In the end, she thought that she had benefited greatly from the "problem," for some lifelong troublesome thoughts had been exposed and healed, and she had grown in her understanding of her spiritual resources.

When problems are dealt with existentially, there is always a twofold benefit. Not only is the specific problem resolved, but the overall spiritual growth and well-being of the individual are increased, and this usually means more to the individual than the disappearance of the problem.

The two intelligent questions heal the marital mistakes and all their negative consequences. Our negativity and externalism, not only in regard to our spouses but in regard to problems themselves, are healed. Negativism leads us to think that a problem is something bad happening to us from outside, and we must make it go away. But a problem is not really something bad, nor is it happening to us from outside. "Problems are lessons designed for our edification," according to Principle 8. Edification means spiritual or moral growth, upbuilding. So, problems are opportunities to learn something important existentially. The truth demonstrates its Reality to us in the resolving of the problem. We need to view life's problems in the same way we view the problems assigned to us in a math class. We may not like having them assigned; some may seem very difficult; yet we do not resent or fight them, because we know that solving them is part of the process of learning math.

Solving life-experience problems is part of the process of learning the laws of health, harmony and good in life. Moreover, just as we can be certain that the math problems, however difficult, are solvable if we learn what we need to know, and that the teacher will help us if we need help, so we can be certain that our marriage problems are resolvable and help available. "God helps those who let him." We can face the problem calmly and confident of a good outcome, and that in itself facilitates the solution enormously.

In the healing of the marital mistakes, we are making it possible for God to help us. Most of us think that we would be glad to let God help us; we may even have been begging him to help us, to no apparent avail. The trouble often is that our prayers are based upon mistaken seeing. We try to get God to fix what's wrong or to make our spouses change or, sometimes, even to punish our partners for what they have "done" to us. Barbara, for instance, thrashed around all night after her fight with Bill, praying desperately, "O God, please help me. Please don't let this happen to me. How could Bill be so mean to me? I'll show him. I'll walk out on him and see how he likes it. O God, please help me. Make Bill love me the way he used to. Don't let me be alone. O God, please!"

God cannot help her with her problem. God can only help her with her seeing, for unless and until things change in her seeing, they cannot change in her experience.

When we turn our attention to the two intelligent questions, we are actually asking God to redefine the situation for us. Simply to ask the questions is to be involved in the perfect problem-solving prayer, for the questions direct our thinking onto the level of healing truth. When we are willing to discover the false beliefs and concerns in our own thinking which make up our part of the problem, and stick to a concern with the healing of our own ignorance, then we have let God help us and we will profit from the "problem." From my own experience, I would say that this is the most important principle in marital problem-solving: *Find your own issue and stick with it.*

Because of the marital mistakes, however, that may be a very, very difficult thing to do. There are some booby traps along the way, and if we are not alert to them, we will become distracted from the path.

One major booby trap is feelings—if not our own, then our spouse's. The marital mistake of negativism of course shows up in negative feelings. You can't think all day about what's wrong without feeling bad. But if you believe your feelings, then you end up reversing the process and saying, "Something must be wrong because I feel so bad." And then you may believe that what's wrong must be "talked out" or "worked on" in some way so that you can stop feeling so bad. That's the fallacious line of reasoning which underlies the popular emphasis on exploring and verbalizing feelings.

The constructive response to feelings is neither to suppress nor to express them, but to understand them. They are pointers to the mental mistakes we are making, and we can be healed of both the bad feelings and the mental mistakes if we use feelings for our edification rather than believing them. If Barbara had been able to say, when anxiety and rage welled up in her at Bill's announcement, "Wow, I'm feeling terribly upset; I don't know what it is, but I have to think about it for a while, because I'm feeling really scared and really mad," she could have learned what she needed to know without having to go through the terrible fight with Bill. A useful motto might be: "Make your feelings be your servants. Don't let yourself become their servants."

But what about somebody else's feelings? What do we do if our husbands or wives confront us with an emotional outburst? We do the same thing that we do with our own feelings: look for the mental issue, in which we must have some share ourselves, and seek to see the Reality of the situation. We get off the track usually because we think that we have to "handle" the other individual's feelings. We think that because we take their feelings personally. Then we feel like the target, and nobody likes to be "shot at" emotionally. So we become involved in either trying to make the individual suppress his feelings by putting them down ("Oh, you're just making a fuss over nothing") or we try to defend ourselves from the feelings by counterattacking. That's what Bill did when Barbara exploded at him. He felt attacked and reacted with a bigger and better explosion. But neither a putdown nor a counterattack works very well: both tend to add fuel to the fire, and bitterness and blaming remain on both sides.

It is possible to simply bow out of the target role, and that can be done, even when the other individual is "aiming right at" you. The secret lies in your own thinking. It is a matter of where your attention is fixed. A concern with yourself at such a moment insures that you will take the other's feelings personally. That self-concern tacks you right up on the wall as a target. But if your concern is to allow the light of God's Reality to reveal the ideas which are making such a hullabaloo so that you can respond helpfully, you literally disappear emotionally from the scene.

Nobody can make us a target; it is a voluntary position. We assume it the moment we become defensive. The
"art of self-defense" is, when viewed existentially, a "commitment to targethood." This is the existential principle
underlying Jesus' seemingly incomprehensible injunction to
"turn the other cheek" (Luke 6:29). It is the secret of his
own mysterious capacity to simply "pass through the
midst" of a hostile crowd which was preparing to push him
over a cliff (Luke 4:30).

Negative emotions interact with negative emotions. If
an individual, confronted with such a display, sees through
the emotions rather than giving them reality and importance by reacting to them, they lose their power. The one
who sees through becomes himself "transparent"—absent
as a target. And the emotions, failing to find confirmation,
tend to lose their "punch." Usually the upset simply fades
away.

We cannot rescue someone from his or her ego trip by
joining him or her. Over the years, Jan and I have developed a practice of "staying out of each other's movies," and
it has proven to be a wonderful tool for growth and harmony in the marriage. We discovered it unwittingly, as we
each struggled to stick with valid principles in our life
together, and it worked so well that it has become a consistent practice. When one partner is "out of whack," the
other maintains a respectful distance, giving the troubled
individual room and time to work it out with God. The love
and respect involved in doing this for someone are powerful. They communicate: "I know you are having a hard
time with something, but I am confident that you can
resolve the problem in your consciousness. I'm working
prayerfully to support you." When this is done, instead of
one individual's "movie" becoming a *folie à deux* (double
insanity), the other partner takes it upon himself or herself
to be the channel for the good of God, guaranteeing the

operation of healing, harmonizing spiritual values right in the troubled situation.

Refusing to become a target helps us avoid another major pitfall, and that is blaming our partner. Blaming someone else for our problems is the natural outcome of the marital mistakes, and it is, besides, a deliciously self-confirmatory thing to do. Self-pity and self-righteousness feel very good to the ego, and they thrive in the atmosphere of blame. But blame has two very painful side-effects; it keeps us hooked up to suffering, and it keeps the blamed-one hooked on to mistaken beliefs. The more we observe and suffer from the side-effects, the less appetizing blame becomes.

Dawn, for example, discovered that her husband Jack had been to bed with another woman while he was away on a business convention across the country. Jack himself was very embarrassed and remorseful, it having been a momentary lapse resulting from his over-indulgence in alcohol and his over-zealous concern to "go along" with the antics of the customer he was wooing. He apologized to Dawn, begged her forgiveness, and gave evidence of having learned something.

But Dawn felt so hurt by his behavior that she would not let it go. Her ego told her that Jack had done something Very Bad to her and that it was Important, it *mattered*. Maybe it was enough for Jack to just shrug it off with an apology, but Dawn was not about to drop the matter so easily. In some vague way, blaming Jack made her feel one-up on him; he owed her something, and she was going to hang onto the debt. In interaction thinking, it's always handy to have an IOU stashed away. And so, unwittingly, Dawn clung to her hurt; she not only clung to it, she intensified it. The bigger the hurt, the bigger the IOU. Eventually, Jack decided that as long as he was being thought of as an unfaithful husband, he might as well be one, and the marriage eventually dissolved amid bitter recriminations on both sides. Blaming is a commitment to suffering and ignorance and it never—what, never? . . . no, never—does anybody any good.

When we focus on the two intelligent questions, we are freed from the personalizing which lies at the heart of blaming. We recognize that the troublemaker is ignorance—the sea of mental garbage—and not somebody. And when we recognize that, we can allow the mental garbage which has crept into our own thinking to be washed away, and we can also forgive our spouse's behavior. Indeed, knowing that it is not the true being of our loved one which is deliberately doing something negative, but the activity of a false belief which is at work, we not only can forgive, but we can ally ourselves secretly with his or her spiritual identity to work constructively against the offending beliefs.

I once read a very moving testimony by a father whose teenage son seemed lost in the world of drugs. The father, unable to communicate directly with his son, began, as he put it, to "have long talks with the boy's angel." Eventually the boy was healed, and father and son could talk together directly again. The father did not explain what he meant by talking with his son's angel, but it seemed to involve a continuing acknowledgment of the boy's pure, spiritual identity as present, untouched by the physical appearances, and responsive to intelligence and love.

If our husbands or wives are in the grip of self-defeating, destructive thoughts, they need our help, not our blame. And we can help by refusing to identify them with those thoughts and by clinging steadfastly to the knowledge that their true being is God-given and God-governed. (That's what God is seeing.) If we cannot talk to them, then we talk to their angels. That's problem-solving. And that's love.

Most people divorce because they are fooled by the marital mistakes into thinking that marriage problems are an indication that there is something wrong with the marriage. That is simply not true. There is nothing wrong with marriages, only with our ideas about marriage . . . and life . . . and ourselves and others. Problem-solving is the very essence of intelligent living. It is the process of uncovering the troublesome beliefs which plague mankind and allowing the spiritual truth of Reality to dissolve them. That is a wonderful, rewarding and fulfilling process in which to participate. To allow one's consciousness to be a channel through which light is shed and suffering healed is the most creative and beneficial activity possible to man.

And so, marital problem-solving, as we are considering it, turns into an extraordinary spiritual discipline, a continual exercise in ego-transcendence. The "forever-twoness" of marriage, which can give rise to such acute feelings of desperation, is a continual spur toward the realization of the unity which we find in God, whenever we break through the ego-lie. And, breaking through the ego-lie is what problem-solving is all about. The essence of effective problem-solving is letting go of the problem mentally, and in order to do that we must let go of all the ego-considerations which gave rise to and support the problem.

Easy, it's not; valuable, it is. For we do not solve our problems just for our own sakes, though we are the first to benefit from it. Every problem dissolved benefits the entire human race. It may seem to be just a matter of getting over a personal snit about, say, your husband or wife staying out late after a class or meeting. But if that snit is resolved by existential insight, then it contributes to far more than just your marriage. Every time truth exposes falsehood, light dissolves darkness, intelligence and love replace ego and ignorance, and the collective consciousness of mankind is improved.

And starting fresh, as from a second birth,
Man, in the sunshine of the world's new spring,
Shall walk, transparent, like some holy thing.

Thomas Moore

SUMMARY

"God helps those who let him" (Principle 5 of Meta-psychiatry).

"Problems are lessons designed for our edification" (Principle 8 of Metapsychiatry).

• Three marital mistakes—negativism, externalism and personalism—lie at the heart of marital problems. The correcting of these mistakes is required for the genuine healing of the problems.

• These mistakes are corrected as we concern ourselves with asking the "two intelligent questions":
1. What is my mental issue here—the lesson I need to learn?
2. What is the Reality of the situation? (What is God seeing?)

• When we ask these questions, we are making it possible for God to help us in the only way possible: by redefining the situation in the light of God's Reality.

• "Problems are lessons designed for our edification." They are the way Life alerts us to the presence of mental garbage in our thinking, so that we can become free from it and its negative fruits.

• The existential resolving of a problem not only removes the problem, but contributes to the enlightenment of the individual and the overall improvement of human consciousness.

EXISTENTIAL THINK-WORK SHEET

When attempting to respond intelligently to a "problem," here are some ideas to consider.

1. Am I stuck on the level of the problem, mentally wrestling with it all the time?

    . . . Problems can never be overcome by wrestling with them. They can only be dissolved by the light of truth. If your child is afraid of dragons in the dark, you don't fight the dragons; you turn on the light.

2. Am I feeling overwhelmed by bad feelings?

    . . . You don't have to believe the feelings. They are not *your* feelings; they are an idea's feelings. And both the feelings and the idea which they are manifesting belong to the "sea of mental garbage" and not to you or your life.

3. Am I thinking that the solution to the problem lies in the future, *if* and *when* certain things happen?

    . . . The solution is always *now*, in the spiritual dimension in consciousness. Everything real that is ever going to be already is.

4. Am I taking myself *very* seriously? (Poor me! Tragic hero/heroine, center stage, spotlight.)

    . . . A good belly laugh has been known to save lives. Consider the Zen monk who, upon becoming enlightened, laughed for two days and two nights.

5. Am I trying to manage my life in some way in an attempt to solve or escape the problem?

    . . . The idea of self-management is itself a problem. Your life is none of your business.

6. Am I believing that someone else has to change before my problem can be solved?

    . . . Find your own issue and stick with it. Nobody can bug you unless you invite it—and as long as you invite it, you'll always find people to bug you.

Problems are lessons for our edification.* In them, Life shows us the old, false, limiting ideas which are interfering with our freedom, our joy, our wholeness, the blooming of our lives. Welcome the opportunity to replace those old ideas with the truth, and the problem ends up blessing your life.

* Thomas Hora. *Dialogues in Metapsychiatry* (New York: Seabury Press, 1977), p. 230. This is Principle 8 of Metapsychiatry.

8. Marriage
and the Single Eye

"If you know what, you know how" (Principle 6 of Metapsychiatry).

"If therefore thine eye be single, thy whole body shall be full of light" (Matthew 6:22).

The Revised Standard Version of the Bible translates the word "single" in the above quotation as "sound." That is an interesting and helpful translation: if our seeing is sound and healthy, then our bodies will be full of light, that is, the "body" of our experience will be healthy. Yet the earlier translation, from the King James Version, suggests a dimension missing from the other, one which is very instructive for a discussion of marriage. To speak of the "single eye" is to speak of an inner spiritual focus, a single-minded seeing beyond the appearances. And it is particularly pointed to speak of the "single" eye in marriage, with its emphasis on doubleness. In no other life situation is it more important, or more difficult, to maintain a single eye than it is in marriage. The single eye sees God. And God is the health, the soundness, the unity of our marriages.

Polly Berends writes:

> Since "beauty is in the eye of the beholder," it is
> the eye that must be trained, first to see, then to
> see beauty. Ultimately there is another eye alto-
> gether with which to see. The real objective in the
> quest for beauty is the discovery of this eye. To
> see anything beyond the tip of one's . . . nose, to
> see beyond the surface of a picture, beyond diffi-
> cult circumstances and seemingly ugly personal-
> ities of this life are all steps toward this objective.
>
> What is important about this is not only what we
> see . . . when we see . . . with the inner eye . . . but
> even more what we become in the moment of
> inner seeing. In such an instant we become what
> we truly are—one with the One Mind, one with
> the infinite qualities of the One Mind. . . . When
> we perceive order, we become orderly; when we
> perceive harmony, we become harmonious. Per-
> ceiving spiritual reality, our lives become spiritual,
> leaving no room for material discomfort or lack.
> Perceiving oneness we become one, leaving no
> room for dualistic conflict of any sort. Perceiving
> truth, we become truthful; perceiving beauty, we
> become beautiful.[1]

The Bible says, "A man leaves his father and his
mother and cleaves to his wife, and they become one flesh"
(Genesis 2:24). The unity of the flesh does not, of itself,
bring about a genuine unity, a oneness of mind and spirit.
That unity is ours, in the sometimes desperate doubleness

1. Polly Berrien Berends, *Whole Child, Whole Parent* (New York: Harper's Magazine
   Press), p. 148.

of marriage, only as we seek the single eye, the perception of our oneness in God.

Individuals often feel caught between the claims of self and the demands of others: this is the "porcupine" bind. We feel driven to seek unity in marriage by trying to make our partner conform to our ideas; when that is impossible, we may feel driven to seek freedom from friction and the pursuit of self-concerns by becoming "single" again. But one does not need to be unmarried in order to become "single" in the existential sense. What we really need is a single-minded concern with spiritual seeing, for when we see things spiritually, we find frictionless unity in marriage and confident, unassailable individual identity. Only the single eye can yield both for us at the same time.

It takes time to find and to maintain the single eye. It is simply impossible to keep focused beyond the ego, in the distractions of our lives together, if that focus is not found and nurtured and cherished in quiet times apart from the din.

By now, hopefully, it is clear that seeing is the most important issue of our lives. "As thou seest, so thou beest." We cannot be real until we can see Reality, and our lives and our marriages cannot be healthy, happy, harmonious, unless they are real.

We have to learn to see spiritually. Nobody is born automatically seeing spiritual Reality; even Jesus regularly took times apart to nourish his spiritual perception. The process of being "born again" is a process, and, as discussed in Chapter 1, it is a process of learning to become consciously aware of—to recognize—the intangible spiritual Reality which lies beyond the reach of the physical senses and intellectual reasoning. We all are equipped with the "single eye," the capacity to "attain higher levels of consciousness and to behold Reality in its spiritual dimension." But it is a faculty which needs to be consciously actualized and developed. It is more important to develop than any other capacity, for we cannot realize existential fulfillment apart from spiritual discernment.

There is no best or only way to develop the single eye. Almost every religious, spiritual or human-potential group of which I know purports to have the best, or the only way, but that simply cannot be true. If there were one way of spiritual realization which was far superior to others, it would have proven itself with legions of enlightened individuals over the centuries or years. None has. So we need to beware of promises of quick or easy enlightenment. No technique in the whole world can, of itself, promise or supply spiritual seeing. Enlightenment cannot be "done," so it is not a matter of technique.

Principle 6 of Metapsychiatry, "If you know what, you know how," was formulated to speak to the concern with techniques. It answers the question "How do I learn to see spirituallly?" It points to the fact that spiritual growth takes place when interest leads an individual to seek to know the nature of Reality—what really is. The more one begins to understand what is, the less the question "how" arises.

Growing into spiritual discernment is somewhat like learning to appreciate art or music. If I become interested in modern art, for instance, I will want to learn to see in it what the experts see. In the beginning, all I see is a bunch of blobs of paint. Yet I hear others talking about seeing all sorts of other things in the same painting. If I want to be able to see what they see, then I begin to pursue the matter. I take a class on modern art, I read books about the subject, I visit museums and spend time looking at modern art works. Perhaps I even seek out a modern artist and ask him or her to tell me about the art. Gradually, as others point out the intangible realities of balance, space, light and shade, color, etc., I become able to see things which were invisible to me before. If my interest continues, I will reach the point where I can, on my own, discern the aesthetic realities of modern art; perhaps, because of my individuality, I even become able to enrich others' discernment by my particular appreciation.

Clearly, the essential aspect of learning to understand modern art is interest. That interest itself leads me to find and use the available resources for the growth in seeing which I seek. Nowhere along the line is the question "How do I learn to appreciate modern art?" relevant. If I am interested, I seek and I find and I learn.

This is an important implication of the word "single" in the biblical quote. My whole body is filled with light only if my eye is single. Like Jesus' comment about the impossibility of serving two masters, his teaching here reminds us that spiritual vision comes about only as a consequence of single-minded interest. We have to be *more* interested in learning to see spiritually than in becoming lost in the material, personal and interpersonal distractions which bombard us from all sides. If we are so interested, then we find that we long for quiet times apart, to center our attention on that realm which is "altogether lovely." Just as a refreshing shower is no chore, but a delight when we are hot and dusty, so the refreshment of beholding spiritual unity and goodness, when our minds are exhausted from the tiresome mental hassle of personal and interpersonal concerns, is welcomed and sought.

Individuals will find different forms of meditation and prayer particularly useful. The two classic forms of meditation consist of non-content meditation and content meditation, which in metapsychiatry is termed prayer. It is mostly Eastern religions which have traditionally practiced non-content forms of meditation. The most prevalent in our Western culture today are Zen meditation and Transcendental Meditation. TM is the most widespread and the simplest to incorporate into a busy daily schedule.

The purpose of non-content meditation, in which consciousness is centered on one's breathing, a mantra, a koan, a chant or some visual image, is to disconnect one's attention from the repetitious, ego-dominated thought processes. This is always a very relaxing thing for the body and mind. Ultimately, when followed in a very disciplined manner, under the guidance of an enlightened teacher, non-content meditation can lead to a breakthrough from ego-consciousness to transcendental awareness for some people.

Christian tradition has tended more to stress content meditation: focusing the attention on the contemplation of a certain phrase or image which points to Reality, such as "Be still and know that I am God" or "The Lord is my shepherd; I shall not want." One ponders this statement, holding attention on it until other thoughts are quieted. Metapsychiatry particularly recommends this kind of meditation in the form of "the prayer of beholding."[2] In the chapter on "Meditation" in the *Dialogues*, Dr. Hora states:

> We have to clarify several phases of meditation. The first phase is prayer, which is verbal. We can talk to ourselves, perhaps making an affirmation such as "God is Love," reciting a psalm or the Lord's Prayer, or reading a passage in the Bible.

> The second phase is non-verbal and this is called contemplation, where we are getting more and more quiet and are contemplating the nature of divine reality non-verbally. Contemplation proceeds to the point of beholding, (which is) knowing, reaching beyond thought. Then comes the third phase which is beyond words and thoughts.

2. See Thomas Hora, *Existential Metapsychiatry, op. cit.,* Chapter 4, as well as index references to "prayer" in the *Dialogues*.

It is absolute stillness, awareness, listening and hearing. Then there is PAGL (peace, assurance, gratitude, love). And when PAGL comes, we know that we have journeyed into the kingdom of God, into spiritual awareness.

All valid forms of prayer and meditation are "journeys into the kingdom of God," however that journey and that kingdom are termed. We seek to see and know Reality beyond the grubby confines of the ego, and when we see and know that Reality, we find God.

It is my experience that in addition to non-content forms of meditation, for those who choose those forms, some kind of "spiritual study" regularly is very helpful. We are enormously blessed to have the "reports" of those who have, over the centuries, seen beyond the ego. Recognizing that words are inadequate to report that which lies beyond words and thought, nonetheless, there is great encouragement, support and facilitation of spiritual seeing to be found in reading regularly the Bible and other spiritual literatures, including individual testimonies of healing and enlightenment.[3]

Setting aside some time each day for quiet thought, study, meditation and prayer is a very spiritually nourishing practice. It seems especially important that we provide ourselves with some time alone in silence. Our culture is overflowing with individuals who seemingly cannot tolerate quiet. Even when walking, jogging or riding bicycles, they provide themselves with radio noise. Every camping

---

3. Three sources of first-hand accounts of trans-ego perceptions include the regular weekly and monthly periodicals of Christian Science, which feature healing testimonies in every issue and are always available at any Christian Science reading room; the book *Three Pillars of Zen*, which has a section of enlightenment testimonies; and the *Commentaries on Living*, Third Series, by J. Krishnamurti (Wheaton, Ill.: The Theosophical Publishing House).

trip we have had, except for one, has been marred by the presence of people who seem to require that they open their car doors, tune in a rock station, and turn the radio up as loud as it will go.

What's the matter with loud rock music? It is not the music, but the avoidance of, the incapacity for, silence which is the problem. Spiritual reality cannot be discerned if one's consciousness is kept distracted by sounds. The addiction to noise reveals an anxiety about one's mental contents; many people are terrified of their "inner noise"— the thoughts and feelings and fantasies belonging to their ego-consciousness. But that "inner noise" can be stilled; it must be stilled if we are to be available to that which constitutes our true being, resources, and reality.

For people unused to silence, the first attempts at sitting quietly may be anxiety-producing. One may feel panicky, or one's mind may be flooded with ideas of things that must be done right then. When anxiety is present, it is helpful to find a comforting text and read it over until one feels more calm. The principles of metapsychiatry make excellent meditation guides. Such phrases as "The good of God ... already is" or simply "Everything is already all right" are very reassuring and centering.

It is important to keep all "shoulds" out of spiritual practice. You do not take time because you "should"; there is no particular thing you "should" or "should not" be thinking, feeling, doing, etc. If we are interested in seeing spiritually, we want to find and use helpful pointers, and we try out suggestions, using those which prove most useful to us. There is no "success" or "failure" involved, because spiritual seeing is not a personal achievement. Our study, prayer and meditation times are times of appreciating what already is, not times of personal striving to accomplish something that is not yet.

In a sense, then, we do not take our individual discipline too seriously. Since we understand that there is no technique which of itself yields spiritual seeing, we do not let a technique become a compulsive, ego-dominated ritual. I have known spiritual students who had anxiety attacks if something in their schedule made it impossible for them to follow their usual practice. That anxiety reveals an unhealthy belief in the magical power of a technique, a preoccupation with control of one's spiritual growth—in short, self-confirmatory thinking. But the good of God already is. Our spiritual practice does not make it be. In fact, based on the wrong ideas, spiritual practice can interfere with our realization of what already *is*. Interest is interest; compulsivity is not the same. So we do not take our spiritual practice too seriously.

This is particularly important in marriage and family life. A valid spiritual discipline can always be practiced in a way which does not make trouble for everybody else in the family. Things can be arranged so that quiet time is available to everyone without anyone suffering. For example, if one or both parents work a full day and want to take some time apart when they get home before supper, that is entirely reasonable. It is even a good idea. But children do not need to be kept waiting for a late supper if that is difficult for them. The ideal of a family dinner together may have to be sacrificed if it seems more important that parents have quiet time before supper. Or, vice versa, in a family where the family dinner together is a special time of sharing, then the meditation time will be arranged so as not to interfere.

The point is that it is more important for particular spiritual practice to fit in harmoniously with the needs of all family members than that one person keep an arbitrary schedule of some sort. If a practice is not intelligent and considerate, it is not spiritual. If we discover willfulness and rigidity in our practice, then ego is running the show, and we can be certain that the practice isn't going to do us very much good.

What about spiritual practice with children? A mother of small children once asked, "How do you introduce your children to God?" (I was tempted to reply, "You say, 'God, these are my children. Children, meet God.'") We don't ask how to introduce our children to sunshine or beauty or the air we breathe. We simply, automatically, share these things with our children, for they are basic realities in our lives. If we find ourselves wondering how to introduce God to our children, then it is evident that God is like our Uncle George, who lives far away and only occasionally comes for a visit.

What is most important for children is the state of their parents' consciousness. *They live what we see.* It is of no avail for us to try to enforce a belief in something which we do not ourselves really see and understand. In fact, it is actually detrimental to children to have beliefs emphasized which do not correspond to their experience. (I have known parents with a "love-God-or-I'll-slap-you-silly" approach.) If parents are concerned that their children learn something of God, let them develop their own single eye, making sure that their spiritual concern shows up in everyday living.

When parents regularly take time to be alone and commune with God, this makes a powerful impression on children. In our family, "taking time" is something the grown-ups do, and the boys know that during that time we are being quiet with God. They respect that practice and will say to friends, "You gotta be quiet. My dad's taking time." They do not themselves have any formal meditation or prayer practices, beyond our fairly traditional "grace" before meals (usually a song) and bedtime "prayers." They do, however, have times of quiet, sometimes with books or workbooks or craft projects, sometimes not. Often one will play quietly alone, and this is encouraged. They do not yet have radios and we do not make it a practice, when riding in the car as a family, to have the radio on. At home, when they do homework, they do it without background radio or TV. Parents who value quiet times for themselves will see to it that the children don't develop the habit of noise. Children may or may not be given special techniques for using quiet time, but in any case the quiet is important for its own sake.

Since prayer is understood to be a concern with seeing God's spiritual Reality, there is a lot of informal prayer in our family all the time. I often verbalize for the boys both my beholdings and my inability to behold. Sometimes I will even ask them for their help. And children can help. Many times, in many ways, our boys have pulled me out of some self-indulgence; reminded me of God's presence, and helped me be spiritually aware. In the spiritual quest, we are all learners, helping one another as we are able. The grown-ups are not big bosses who know it all, trying by dint of their size and authority to make the kids shape up. In fact, I often think of children as our little brothers and sisters, one with us in the life process of learning to know our spiritual Parent.

An important aspect of the single eye in family life is the practice of being mindful of our blessings. For children, this usually means being thankful for their presents, possessions and achievements. That is all right. It is the being thankful that counts. We often include in our bedtime ritual the singing together of the Tallis Canon: "All praise to thee, my God, this night/For all the blessings of the light." We stop at this point and share what the blessings of the day have been, and then continue the song to the end: "Keep me, O keep me, King of Kings/Beneath thine own almighty wings." When such a practice gets stale and no longer thoughtful, we drop it for a while. When the boys began to recite their blessings as: "Salty-God-Jesus-

and-the-angels-and-everything-we-did-today," we thought it time to find a new form for appreciating blessings. (Salty, incidentally, is our dog. I trust that God-Jesus-and-the-angels didn't mind coming second, for Salty is a very loving and intelligent little beast.)

At one time, my husband and I found it very fruitful to end the day by sitting together and sharing the good of our day, mainly what was going on in our spiritual lives. If we had discovered a new text, realized something, or read something helpful, we shared it. Often we would share how we had resolved some seeming problem that had arisen. We usually do not verbalize our difficulties. We don't "talk them out," though sometimes we will ask one another for help. But we have been mindful of the advice given us when we married: "Don't share problems with your spouse; share joy with your spouse. Take your problems to God, or to your psychotherapist." This advice has proven to be very good, indeed. Too often, one's spouse is regarded as the legitimate "dumping ground" for one's problems. But your spouse is not your therapist, even when your spouse is a therapist. It is better to take your problems to God and, if you don't know how to do that, to someone who can teach you how. And then, it is wonderful to share with your husband or wife the resolution of that problem. Jan and I have both, over the years, been strengthened and encouraged and enriched by watching the other face a problem squarely and work it out with God. This is particularly true when the problem is one which could be viewed as an interpersonal problem. There is no time when I feel more grateful for my husband than when I see him turn away from the temptation to hook into some ignorance of mine, take it to God, and come out really free.

This does not mean keeping one's problems to oneself. Men particularly, in our culture, seem to have been raised to think that it is unmanly to admit to having problems, and especially to seek help from someone else. Much marital disharmony is perpetuated by husbands who say, "I don't have a problem; if you do, you can get help for yourself—or you can leave," or "Nobody can tell me how to solve my problems." Problems don't get resolved that way, and wives tend to become alienated by the unconstructive attitude of the husband. Everybody has problems; they are the primary means by which we grow and learn in life. Intelligent response to problems, which includes getting whatever help we may need from others, is not a sign of weakness and it has nothing to do with manhood. It is simply intelligent.

Women traditionally are more open to conscious problem-solving, more willing to change their thinking. But they need to beware, in our day, that they don't change in self-defeating directions. The tendency in popular feminist thought is simply to glorify what used to be considered masculine values: aggressiveness, intellectualism, sexual and professional ambition, etc. Many women today are very, very confused about what is womanly. This confusion can be cleared away only by looking beyond conflicting cultural standards, which are concerned with roles and activities, to spiritual qualities. Whether one is male or female, it is existentially necessary that one be intelligent and loving and concerned with an awareness of spiritual good. We don't make our identities; we cannot calculate our wholeness. We find our identities, our wholeness, in God, and nowhere else.

One of the very interesting ramifications of the single eye in marriage is that it opens up new understandings of what is masculine and what is feminine, enabling husbands and wives to become free from the problem-producing miseducation of their backgrounds and contemporary society. Individuals who are concerned with spiritual seeing will lose a concern with proving themselves in terms of sexual, physical or personal identity. Only spiritual identity matters, and, spiritually, all men and women are complete and they manifest, in individual ways, all spiritual qualities. Unlike the popular "unisex" trend which tends toward seeing men as more feminine and women as more masculine, spiritual identity involves the recognition that both men and women express, in different ways, the basic spiritual values which constitute Reality. Single-eyed men and women think in different terms than the popular ones. They ask not "How will this make me look? Is this a manly/womanly thing to do?" but "Does this reveal the good of God? Is this an intelligent, loving, honest, beautiful, good thing to do?"

Another very important fruit of seeking to see everything in the light of spiritual Reality is that the most mundane household activities become, in a sense, sanctified. We do not focus on one kind of doing as really valuable and resist something else because it is not as important. The value of life lies in our seeing, and when we see clearly, we become free to respond usefully moment-by-moment to the needs of the moment.

There is an oft-told Zen story of two monks who were renowned for their good humor. When people asked them what made them so happy, they replied, "What could be more wonderful than chopping wood and drawing water?" Having established their happiness in the clear realization of their oneness with perfect Life, they found complete joy in the task of the moment, whatever it was.

This example stands in great contrast to our usual experience in marriage and family life, where the simple tasks of the household present endless difficulties to our ego-centered minds. How many of the routine tasks of family life are weighted down with personal and interpersonal issues that make them problematic? And what a waste of time and energy is involved in resisting, resenting and fighting over these tasks. As mentioned in Chapter 2, keeping the simple tasks simple is quite a spiritual discipline in and of itself.

In fact, it is a form of meditation simply to attempt to do one's daily tasks in a state of mental alertness and "thereness." Instead of trying to escape mentally while we are cleaning the house, mowing the lawn or driving to an appointment by having the radio or TV on or fantasizing, we may attempt to be present to the present moment. It is also very edifying to remind oneself as one works that "cleanliness is cleaning, order is making orderly, vitality is being active, intelligence is solving this problem," etc. We are only stressed or aggravated by tasks when we believe that we have to do them; it greatly reduces the stress and strain when we mentally turn the job over to the Reality which is really doing it.

When our seeing is "single," then our whole marriage is full of light, and not only "light" in the sense of clear and wholesome seeing, but "light" in the sense of "lightness," the opposite of "heaviness." The burdensomeness of our work is relieved. More than that, the single eye in marriage also removes the "heaviness" of interpersonal living, the burden of personal concerns. There is a lot of humor, fun, and playfulness because egos are not taking themselves seriously. Genuine humor is both a sign and a prerequisite of healthy living. Genuine humor is distinguished from personal sarcasm or teasing, which are not funny at all, and also from the tyrannical humor of the compulsive joke-maker. Genuine humor is never personal and never compulsive, because it springs from the discernment of the transpersonal, a discernment which reveals, suddenly, the silliness of pretentious ego concerns. It is therefore healing. Norman Cousins discovered the healing consequences of laughter, even without discovering the existential perspective behind it.

It has been my observation in families with a severely disturbed teenager that such families totally lack humor. There is no sense of family fun, of a lighthearted banter between family members. Everything is deadly serious. The parents, of course, assume that they are serious because there is nothing to laugh at. But there is nothing to laugh at because they are so serious.

In a single-eye orientation, we know that nothing of the ego is to be taken with final seriousness, because the ego and its version of Reality is an illusion, a false construct. So, even though things seem real and weighty, we hang loose and keep in mind the Zen monk who, upon becoming enlightened, laughed for two days and two nights. If things are that funny, what are we getting so upset about?

Respect for others in the family does not mean respect for personhood or taking oneself seriously. Therefore, we do not respect feelings, though we respect other people's right to choose what they will do with their feelings. We respect the true being of our spouses and children, their capacities as spiritual children of God.

When our boys are indulging in phony baloney, we say it: "Phony baloney." And they usually look sheepish and grin and then we play around a little. Sometimes, when I find myself starting to slip into arguing with the boys, I'll "put up my dukes" and say,"You want to fight? O. K., let's fight," or I'll assume a pose of a Frankenstein monster and lurch toward them. And usually they laugh and say, "Oh, Mom," in a condescending way, and then we go at the issue again, but in a better frame of mind. The point is to break up my own seriousness, when I become aware of it, and to show the boys that it isn't as big a deal as we've been making it. This is not disrespectful of them, but rather opens up the possibility for all of us to see the "problem" with some distance in order to bring the best of ourselves to it.

Lao Tzu said, "He who feels punctured/Must once have been a bubble." When the single eye is maintained in marriage, there is less tendency to blow oneself up and less danger of getting punctured. The capacity to laugh at ourselves increases as our spiritual seeing grows, and it is a wonderful blessing in marriage.

A marriage in which both partners maintain a single eye becomes an "open marriage" in an existentially valid sense. The popular concept of "open marriage" implies interpersonal openness, allowing partners to get ego "needs" met by other people as well as their spouses. An existential open marriage is one in which the openness is transpersonal. Partners get their needs met in consciousness by God, and thus are able to leave one another free from the stranglehold of interpersonal demands.

As we have noted, however, sometimes ego concerns masquerade as spiritual zeal and end up sabotaging the validity of the practice. In an interpersonally open marriage, there is always the danger that one partner will conclude that someone else provides more goodies than the spouse and will leave the marriage altogether. Something like that is going on in meditation circles where the phrase "Meditate and separate" originated. In that case, individuals get carried away in the excitement and zeal of their particular technique and path and believe that their individual "evolution" by way of that practice is the most important thing in the world. In other words, a technique, a "path," is seen to have more "goodies" to offer than are available in marriage. This is a highly questionable conclusion, simply because it reveals so many elements of ego-concern. It reveals personal ambition, which is no less self-centered because it is supposedly spiritual, and it reveals an ignorance of the absolutely central existential fact that the good of God already is.

There is no "should" involved here. It is not that one

should or should not be married. But it seems important to recognize that it is only when the nature of one's commitment in marriage is misunderstood that marriage presents a problem in the spiritual path. And such a misunderstanding will not be corrected by becoming unmarried.

The commitment in marriage, when it is existentially valid, is not an interpersonal commitment. It is a commitment to the good of God, here discerned, and to the establishing of a life of joint participation in that good. If the marriage was existentially a mistake, based on disintegrative values such as a mutual love of excitement or quest for sexual gratification or whatever, then such a marriage will likely dissolve if only one partner becomes God-centered. But if a marriage was based upon the best that both people knew at that time, then it is not valid for one to decide "I can grow faster on my own" and to leave. The nature of that growth can only be one-sided if it is unable to face up to and transcend the ego-entanglements of marriage. In other words, it may be a lot more fun to whiz off to exotic spots around the world, whenever one chooses, in the pursuit of one's enlightenment, but if that "enlightenment" cannot stand the test of ordinary living, then it is phony.

The openness of a marriage with a single-eyed focus establishes a foundation of singular strength and resiliency. The togetherness is not stifling, the apartness is not threatening. The image of trees standing close together seems apt. Trees may stand very close together without it becoming unhealthy because they draw their life, strength, support and nourishment through their roots, sunk deep in the ground. Likewise, married people find life together both close and frictionless when they cultivate in consciousness an awareness of their Ground of Being and seek their life, strength, support and nourishment there.

> Let thy work appear unto thy servants,
> and thy glory unto their children.

And let the beauty of the Lord our God be upon us:
and establish thou the work of our hands (Psalm 90:16-17).

"If you know what, you know how" (Principle 6 of Metapsychiatry).

"If therefore thine eye be single, thy whole body shall be full of light" (Matthew 6:22).

• In marriage, tension often arises from a seeming conflict between the singleness of individuality and the doubleness of life together. The healing of the tension lies in developing a "single eye," an inner, spiritual focus which sees beyond both false individualities and strained togetherness.

• Genuine unity already is, in divine Being; it is there that we find both our unity in marriage and our true individual identity.

• Spiritual practices—study, prayer, meditation—are a celebration of what *is*, and no such celebration needs to be a source of difficulty for other family members.

• The single eye establishes a genuinely open marriage, in which closeness is frictionless and separation is without anxiety. Seeking to see God's Reality in all that we do, every aspect of our lives becomes sanctified.

9. Open Family

"Call no man your father on earth, for you have one Father, who is in heaven. . . . Who is my mother and who are my brothers? . . . Whoever does the will of my Father in heaven is my brother and sister and mother" (Matthew 12:48, 50; 23:9).

"Show me the face you had before your parents were born" (Zen Koan).

The ephemeral nature of marriage in our time has resulted in shifting family structures which will no doubt change the concept of family ties that has existed up to this time. Presumably, for a child who has a number of step-parents and step-siblings, the belief that "blood is thicker than water" doesn't mean much. Even so, there is today not only a great deal of confusion about what constitutes family, but also a great deal of suffering because of beliefs about family. It therefore seems important to consider the family from an existential point of view. Just as our concept of marriage needs revision, so our concept of family ties, which also is based upon material and interpersonal ideas of man, needs a new perspective.

We have said that marriage is a spiritual partnership, a joint participation in the good of God, a school for spiritual growth. The same things would be true for the larger family as well. If we would come to an existentially valid understanding of the family, then we begin with our definition of life: the meaning and purpose of life is to come to know Reality. If that is what life is all about, then that is what family is all about. Healthy family life is the extension of healthy marriage: a partnership of individuals seeking to understand and grow in spiritual discernment and participate together in the good of God.

Blood ties do not make a family in any significant or valid sense. The essence of family-ness is a genuine sharing of something basic in life. Common material parentage is a very insignificant factor; we all know from our own experience that such material ties do not yield of themselves any genuine "joint participation" over the years. Instead of simply recognizing this as an existential fact and learning from it, however, multitudes, blinded by the belief in the importance of family ties, have suffered greatly from the failure of family to live up to their expectations.

Audrey, for example, the only child of a marriage which ended in divorce, concluded at the time of the split: "I will never have the family I need." Over the years, that believed deprivation has been the focus of her attention, as she has alternately tried to woo step-family members with sweetness and punish them in raging tantrums. Her entire adult life has been dominated by the drive to confirm the failure of family to "meet her needs," and she has thereby not only poisoned the family life which was, but she has remained completely blind to the availability of spiritual resources.

God is our only real family. In God we find our identity, nurture, protection, guidance, intelligence, love, and fulfillment. We are not really determined in any existential sense by the individuals who are our material parents, nor by others who live under the same roof. "Lord, thou has been our dwelling place in all generations" (Psalm 90). We are the spiritual offspring of the One Spiritual Being, and it is in Spiritual Being that we come home to our fulfillment.

When the Zen master asks, "Show me the face you had before your parents were born," he is pointing to the insubstantiality of one's identity based on material lineage. It is only the "person," the counterfeit ego-identity, which is the product of the human family. The more we grow in discernment of our spiritual identities, the less we identify ourselves with the details of family history and the less we are imprisoned in the appearances of physical and psychological inheritances.

Nobody's human family is adequate to meet their needs. Nobody has ever had the perfect childhood, because perfection is not available on the material level of things. When we try to make family life be what it cannot, we end up corrupting what it can be. In the area of the country where we live, cultural trends take somewhat exaggerated form, and it is interesting to note the following. We live in an area of great material abundance with a particular interest in luxury houses, there is a plethora of parenting and family life education courses offered, and the divorce rate is the highest in the country. The families inside of the gorgeous houses are falling apart, in spite of all the how-to-do-it courses for parents. When we look to the wrong place for our resources, we end up bereft.

The fact that we recognize the existential insignificance of "blood ties" does not mean we are advocating the dissolution of the family. We are saying, rather, that the authentic human function of the human family can only be wholesomely exercised when it is an "open family" in the existential sense in which we discussed "open marriage" in the last chapter. The authentic human function of the family is fairly simple and obvious: to provide a structure for the meeting of material needs appropriate to the family members. We need shelter, food, clothing, etc.; little babies need to be taken care of, as do older folk who cannot care for their own material needs. Families are not, however, "supposed" to provide members with everything that they may consider to be needs: approval, support, love, self-confirmation, continued financial and interpersonal supply into adulthood. Most of the problems of parents with grown children stem from the mutual belief that a child has the right to "live off of" his or her parents as long as they live. Parents feel terribly guilty for resenting the continued demands of grown children and often are unable to respond intelligently because of the belief that they are supposed to be their children's resource "forever."

And it works the other way around. Many grown children have problems with parents who believe that their children "owe it to them" to take care of them—in whatever manner they dictate—because of the blood ties. Indeed, that is sometimes suggested as the reason for having children.

Unwittingly, we all are victims of the distortion of family life consequent upon psychological, interpersonal thinking. Seeing other people as the source of our existential supply is always invalid, even if they are our children or our parents. Everybody in the family is better off if we know clearly that we are not and won't even try to pretend to be God. God is God, and it is helpful to learn what that means and to let go of our false sense of responsibility. A recent study of some sort compared children who were defined as "neglected" with those defined as "over-protected" and found that the "neglected" kids were much better off in terms of having discovered and actualized their own resources. Better than neglect, however, is the recognition that God is the Source of supply for all the members of our families, and we are all partners in the quest for fuller realization of our spiritual heritage.

When we know that God is the Parent of us all—of our parents and ourselves and our children—then the roles and functions of human family life take on a simplicity and ease. One is not pushed and pulled and confused by the demands of various family members or by role stereotypes. One's motive stays simple. One does what one does in order to express intelligence, love, generosity, honesty, joy—to make manifest the good of God. That commitment becomes the standard by which decisions are made, freeing us from the conflict and guilt and difficulty which often surround family matters.

The ordinary complexity of family decisions is illustrated by Naomi's situation. She is worried about her mother-in-law, whose physical and mental condition makes twenty-four-hour surveillance, and considerable care, necessary. Naomi is burdened by the belief that she should take her mother-in-law into her home; she feels guilty even mentioning the possibility of having her placed in a nursing facility. Yet when her family situation is examined—she has three small children; her husband is in the middle of a radical professional change which may involve a move to another state; they cannot afford private nursing help—it becomes clear that it is not at all intelligent to think of having her mother-in-law in her home. The woman's needs cannot adequately be met there, and her presence would be disruptive in a family already experiencing the strain of change.

There is a great deal of cultural self-criticism these days because of the pattern of separate facilities for the elderly instead of their being cared for by their children. Cultural factors are argued back and forth, explaining, justifying and/or condemning this trend. That sort of argument goes nowhere. It is riddled with "shoulds" and "should nots" and totally misses out on the existential Reality that the good of God already is and is available to any individual, of any age, in any family situation, in any culture, who looks to God, rather than to relatives, for his or her supply.

My mother, who is eighty-five lives with us. We invited her not out of a sense of family duty, but because, for us and for her, it was a natural unfoldment of good at the time. She brings a quality of presence to our home which is valuable and is appreciated. She is useful in caring for her grandsons, in a limited way, and even more for her unlimited, warm interest in and appreciation of them. We are able to be useful to her by taking care of small tasks which are easy for us but hard for her. We are very grateful that this sharing of good is available to her and to us. The arrangement "works" partly because it is free from any sense of "shoulds" on both sides.

We are most helpful to others when we consistently acknowledge that their lives are governed by Omniactive Love Intelligence, and do not fancy that we are the solution to their problems. Feeling guilty about something is, secretly, a form of bragging: we are saying that we are very important. Even if somebody else would like to believe that, it is not good for them, or for us, if we do. God is very important to us. Period. When our actions are governed by the knowledge that God is running the whole show for everybody, they are likely to be much more life-enhancing and health-producing for everybody concerned.

Being God-centered as a family does not mean being neglectful of mundane matters. Rather, a kind of "yes, but" approach develops. To the newborn infant, a full belly and dry pants are "where it's at." We don't say "no" to that just because we know there's more to life. We say, "Yes, be full and dry," and we see to it that he or she is. But we also mentally provide for his or her existential needs by cherishing the idea of his or her spiritual being and knowing him or her as God's beloved child. At age eight, friends, bikes and OP shorts are "where it's at." "Yes—but all of those good things are forms of God's unlimited goodness." Denial of cherished lesser goods is not necessary; in fact, it only tends to fixate the individual upon that object. Rather, we enjoy such things as pointers beyond themselves, to the boundless good of spiritual Reality.

Our existential obligation is to come to know Reality. Ultimately we can be helpful to others only to the extent that we are in conscious harmony with the truth of being. It is not what we do, but what we know, that is beneficial. "If I give away all I have, and if I deliver my body to be burned, but have not love, I gain nothing" (1 Corinthians 13:3). As loving parents of our children and loving children of our parents, as loving husbands and wives, we need most of all to know the Love that loves all of our loved ones and causes them to bloom, and us as well.

Just as we point beyond ourselves to the Source where all human needs are met, so we look beyond others to that same Source. Our parents did the best that they could, given their degree of understanding at the time. We are grateful for whatever good was present in that human upbringing. That gratitude frees us to move out from our beginning families into life experience, knowing that if we are open to good, it will come, wherever we are, with whomever we may be. In this state of consciousness, something wonderful happens. We discover our "existential" family. We find "spiritual fathers and mothers and sisters and brothers" along the way, individuals with whom we share special bonds of common love and interest at the level of our realization at the time. As we continue to grow, we may grow beyond or apart from some of these individuals. That's what "open family" means. It means that when the focus is on God, one does not need to cling to any family member as the supposed only source of some goodness. As one appreciates and enjoys the good qualities in whoever makes up one's current "family," a continued flow of motherliness, fatherliness, sisterliness and brotherliness takes place. And it is those qualities which make up family, not a particular hunk of flesh labeled "father" or "mother."

Much of the suffering experienced by so-called "adopted" children and "adoptive" parents could be relieved if it were seen that we are all "adopted" when it comes to human family. Our true Mother and Father is God, and the particular form by which we end up with our custodial parents isn't important. Because God is our Parent, motherliness and fatherliness can always be ours the moment we stop looking to certain human persons to supply these qualities.

In an open family, family members who are on different levels of consciousness go different ways and find others who share their levels of thought. There is no need to cling to individuals with whom we share nothing, to make continued demands upon them, or to blame them for not meeting our expectations. This doesn't mean that there is no contact possible. Indeed, when family contacts can be free of interpersonal manipulations, judgmentalism and demands, contact can be very pleasant and positive for everybody. An open family is always free to come close together because such closeness is never imprisoning or strained or full of friction.

The openness of our family is a matter of our own consciousness. We do not have to insist that all of our relatives understand this. There will always be very unenlightened relatives, people who try to cling or demand or judge or blame. We can respect their right to be where they are, in consciousness, without being governed by their invalid concerns. If we realize that we don't have to change them in order to be free, we will be much less disturbed by their ways. As noted in Chapter 3, it is our own interaction thinking which really keeps us interpersonally imprisoned, not other people's demands.

Like marriage, human family life requires the sanctification of spiritual focus if it is to enjoy its true dimensions. And, like marriage, when the focus is taken off the family and turned to God, the structure does not dissolve; it is strengthened and revived. It becomes possible to be a happy family, to have several generations living under one roof if that is appropriate, and to participate in all the rich and joyful experiences of family life on all levels. Spiritual seeing never deprives anyone of any aspect of wholesome experience on any level. Our human lives bloom under the nurture of conscious contact with spiritual Reality.

SUMMARY

• The nature and purpose of family life are defined by the existential definition of life: to come to know Reality.

• The existential definition of family is: a partnership of individuals seeking to understand and grow in spiritual discernment and to participate together in the good of God.

• Blood-ties do not produce family, and we are not limited to material family members for our "supplies" of motherliness, fatherliness, sisterliness and brotherliness. God is our only real family. When we look to God for all good, we discover our larger, existential family, and are supplied with spiritual mothers, fathers and siblings along the way.

• Thus, a valid understanding of family results in an "open family" structure in which we don't cling to, demand from, or blame our relatives. All are free to grow and find "family" with others on the same levels of consciousness. This also leaves room for frictionless contacts, whenever they are appropriate.

10. The Singles' Situation

"The enlightened man neither marries nor does not marry"
(Hora).

What is the situation of the unmarried individual, from an existential point of view? Certainly, a radical redefinition of marriage has consequences for the unmarried individual as well, since his or her situation is largely defined by the prevailing views on marriage.

The cultural beliefs about people and life which we have discussed so far in connection with marriage, show up equally clearly in the so-called "singles' scene," which is receiving considerable attention nationally at this time. There are marked changes taking place, particularly in the way women view marriage and being unmarried, but the changes are the usual cultural swing from one extreme to the other and do not represent an enlightened change of basic premise.

Until the feminist upsurge a few years ago, being unmarried was clearly considered to be an advantage for a man—a "bachelor"—and a disadvantage for a woman—an "old maid." Being a bachelor was glamorous; being an old maid was a humiliation and a deprivation. This had to do with the myth that a man did the choosing, while a woman was chosen—or unchosen. Moreover, the belief prevailed that feminine fulfillment lay solely in being a wife and mother, whereas being a husband and a father were a kind of avocation of men, who fulfilled themselves by way of their career. Never mind that in actual experience none of this was true. It was culturally believed. And so, women supposedly tried to "trap" men into marriage so that they could be fulfilled, and men supposedly tried to escape being "trapped," the better to express their basically lustful and free-roaming natures.

Feminist thought has uncovered part of the nonsense but gone along with the rest of it. It has said, in effect, "What is true for men is equally true for women." So now women also may view marriage, and especially motherhood, as a "trap" which limits their personal fulfillment.

For those men and women who fall for such beliefs, the singles' scene is "swinging"—the most desirable lifestyle, in which optimal personal freedom is coupled with a veritable feast of interpersonal "goodies" just there for the "picking." A man told me of a divorced male business associate who bragged that he bedded a different woman every night and loved it and would continue to do so "as long as my body holds out."

Clearly discernible under such a preoccupation is the ego-view of things, with its inherent problems of self-gratification versus the need for interpersonal produce. The swingers come down on the side of "freedom-to-do-my-thing" and the interpersonal aspect is seen as "freedom-to-get-whatever-I-can-from-whomever-I-can-whenever-I-can." The autonomy of self is glorified with its "freedoms."

Singlehood, however, continues to be an anguish for many people, even for some of those who pretend to be swingers. The belief that human fulfillment is consequent upon being deeply and permanently loved by someone, and deeply and permanently in love with someone, remains embedded in our cultural consciousness. Being single is experienced as being "alone," meaning unchosen, unwanted, and unloved—and this even by some men. Never-married people, especially women, tend to feel essentially flawed; divorced people tend to feel grief and failure and inadequacy. The intense preoccupation of unmarried people with how to meet the "right person" reveals the desperate concern to get established in the supposed security and self-esteem of doubleness. Many singles feel pinched between the drive to do something to find somebody and the unpleasantness of most of the available established ways of meeting other unmarried people. There are many complaints by both men and women that they do not find, at singles' bars or in groups, the kind of people they would really want to marry, but they go there anyway because "where else do you go?"

To this question, metapsychiatry replies, "Don't go—know!" If being unmarried is regarded as a problem, it needs to be approached in the same way that any other problem is approached—as a lesson, an opportunity to grow.

Being unmarried is, from an existential viewpoint, no problem. Being unmarried does not mean that an individual is in any way deprived of anything necessary: love, support, guidance, even companionship. That is because being unmarried is not an existential state, only an interpersonal state. That is, it is only on an interpersonal level that there is any difference between a married and an unmarried individual. It is purely a matter of details and arrangements of life style; it is not an ultimate reality.

Whether an unmarried individual glories in or grieves over his or her state, the focus on singlehood needs to be healed. It is nothing special, one way or the other. And the focus on it, as a positive or a negative thing, forms a block in consciousness to the harmonious, healthy unfoldment of that individual's life. It is not up to us to say whether we should or should not be married. It is up to us to seek to know the good of God, which already is, and allow that good to unfold to us the details.

I was single until I was in my mid-thirties, in a time when it was universally considered to be a stigma. I wrestled with and suffered from all the cultural opinions as I considered myself both flawed and deprived. Every contact with every man was thrown out of focus by the issue of marriage, always lurking in the back of my mind. I was healed of that terrible preoccupation by the following words: "Whether you are married or unmarried, you are always alone with God." When I realized that marriage would not in any way alter my existential situation, I was able to let go of it as an issue, focusing, instead, on learning to find my peace and security in God. Once I had let go of the issue of marriage, it was unfolded to me. And I found, then, that it was not easy to marry; it was very frightening to let go of the reins of my life, opening it up to the uncalculable influences of another individual. But I was aided by, enabled by, those same words which made clear to me that it is God who holds the reins of my life, not me or my husband.

The statement that "the enlightened man neither marries nor does not marry" points out that marriage, in conventional terms, exists only on the interpersonal level. On that level, where it is seen as very important, it becomes either a god or a devil, and we are driven either to pursue or to fight against it. We either marry or do not marry.

But the enlightened individual sees the essential unity of all being, so that he or she does not feel at all separate or lonely. Enlightenment is exactly the realization of oneness with all that is. In the moment of transcendental seeing, the illusions of autonomous selfhood, of singleness, separateness, etc., fade, and one understands the "togetherness" of all Life, in which individuality does not involve any separation from the whole. There is, therefore, no need to try to solve the "problem" of singleness with the "solution" of doubleness. And so, the enlightened man does not concern himself with marriage. He concerns himself with conscious harmony, with perfect Life; he takes what comes and responds intelligently, neither grabbing nor pushing away. If marriage unfolds, it unfolds; if it does not, it does not; he is not concerned either way. Whether he is married or unmarried, he is always alone with God, an "aloneness" which implies undistracted unity, perfect wholeness.

Hopefully, by now, it is clear that this does not mean that an enlightened individual is aloof, cold or withdrawn in marriage. Quite the contrary, he is free to be wholly present to all aspects of married life. Marriage, like breathing, is best when least thought about. All the goods of married life are the by-products of the enlightened consciousness of the partners. They do not come about by a preoccupation with the relationship and making it yield good. They come about when a concern with the relationship, per se, is lost in the beholding of spiritual good.

Unmarried individuals need to lose interest in being unmarried. It is a situation neither of loss nor of license. It is, like all life situations, simply an opportunity to learn and grow. Whether one is divorced or never married, it is no accident. We have always invited our life experience and, rather than seeking to alter it, it behooves us to seek first to understand the invitation.

When we are willing to learn the lessons of our experience, we can be sure that we will be blessed. We can be absolutely certain that Life will never deprive us of any wholesome aspect of living if we concern ourselves with realizing the truth of being. So we don't need to seek for a mate in unwholesome surroundings, subject ourselves to degrading or humiliating experiences, or worry and fret and feel lonely and deprived. The good of God, being spiritual, is boundless. When we involve ourselves mentally with spiritual good, good also takes form in our lives in fulfilling and happy ways.

Marriage is none of your business, one way or the other. "Your Father knoweth that ye have need of these things. . . . Fear not."

SUMMARY

• Whether you are married or unmarried, you are always alone with God.

• Marriage is an interpersonal arrangement, not an existential reality. Therefore a mental preoccupation with being unmarried, whether one glories or grieves over it, is a block to a consciousness of spiritual good.

• Existentially, the situation of the unmarried individual is the same as the situation of the married individual.

• Therefore, "Take no thought for (whether you should be married or unmarried), but seek ye first to know the good of God, which already is." It then becomes possible for marriage to unfold to you as a manifestation of that good.